American Impressionists Abroad and at Home

American Impressionists Abroad and at Home

Paintings from the Collection of The Metropolitan Museum of Art

H. Barbara Weinberg and Susan G. Larkin

This catalogue has been published in conjunction with *American Impressionists Abroad and at Home: Paintings from the Collection of The Metropolitan Museum of Art*, an exhibition organized by The Metropolitan Museum of Art and the American Federation of Arts.

The American Federation of Arts is a nonprofit art museum service organization that provides traveling art exhibitions and educational, professional, and technical support programs developed in collaboration with the museum community. Through these programs, the AFA seeks to strengthen the ability of museums to enrich the public's experience and understanding of art.

Publication Coordinator: Michaelyn Mitchell
Book Design: Eileen Boxer
Editor: Fronia W. Simpson
Printed in Hong Kong

Front cover: Childe Hassam, *Peach Blossoms–Villiers-le-Bel* (detail), ca. 1887–89 (no. 10)
Page 2: Edmund C. Tarbell, *Across the Room* (detail), ca. 1899 (no. 34)
Page 6: Edmund C. Tarbell, *Still Life: Vase of Peonies* (detail), ca. 1925 (no. 27)
Page 10: Frank W. Benson, *Children in Woods* (detail), 1905 (no. 38)

Published in 2000 by the American Federation of Arts, 41 East 65th Street,
New York, New York 10021. www.afaweb.org

Photographs are supplied by the owners of the works and are reproduced by their permission.

Library of Congress Cataloging-in-Publication Data
Weinberg, H. Barbara (Helene Barbara), 1942–
    American impressionists abroad and at home : paintings from the collection of the
    Metropolitan Museum of Art / H. Barbara Weinberg and Susan G. Larkin.
        p. cm.
    Published in conjunction with an exhibition organized by the Metropolitan Museum of Art
    and the American Federation of Arts and held at the San Diego Museum of Art and four other
    museums between Jan. 26, 2001 and June 16, 2002.
    Includes bibliographical references and index.
    ISBN 1-885444-15-X
    1. Impressionism (Art)—United States—Exhibitions. 2. Painting, American—Exhibitions.
3. Artist colonies—France—Influence—Exhibitions. 4. Painting—New York (N.Y.)—
Exhibitions. 5. Metropolitan Museum of Art (New York, N.Y.)—Exhibitions. I. Larkin,
Susan G., 1943– II. Metropolitan Museum of Art (New York, N.Y.) III. American Federation
of Arts. IV. San Diego Museum of Art. V. Title.

ND210.5.I4 W458 2000
759.13'074'7471—dc21   00-044201

Exhibition Itinerary
San Diego Museum of Art
San Diego, California
January 26–April 22, 2001

Delaware Art Museum
Wilmington, Delaware
May 11–August 5, 2001

Cheekwood Museum of Art
Nashville, Tennessee
August 24–November 18, 2001

Orlando Museum of Art
Orlando, Florida
December 7, 2001–March 3, 2002

New York State Museum at Albany, NY
Albany, New York
March 22–June 16, 2002

Contents

Foreword

The American Impressionists were among the most thoroughly trained, widely traveled, and cosmopolitan painters in the history of our nation's art. They recognized in French Impressionism a lively alternative to the refined technique and idealized subject matter prescribed by the European and American academies in which they had studied. The most talented of them grasped the essence of the new French painting—that art should originate in personal experience—and adopted not just its surfaces but its very sum and substance.

American Impressionists Abroad and at Home is the eighth exhibition to result from an ongoing partnership between The Metropolitan Museum of Art and the American Federation of Arts that was designed to share portions of the Metropolitan's collection with museums around the country. Included are thirty-nine paintings that are regularly on view in the galleries or in the Henry R. Luce Center for the Study of American Art, or that have been on long-term loan to other institutions.

First and foremost, our gratitude goes to H. Barbara Weinberg, the Museum's Alice Pratt Brown Curator of American Paintings and Sculpture, and Susan G. Larkin, a former Chester Dale Fellow and the research associate for this project, for their judicious selection of the works in the exhibition and their expert authorship of the catalogue.

For their valuable contributions to the exhibition and this publication, we wish to acknowledge the following additional staff members at the Metropolitan Museum: Dana Pilson and Catherine Scandalis, administrative assistants in the Department of American Paintings and Sculpture; Deanna D. Cross in the Photo and Slide Library; Dorothy Mahon, paintings conservator, and Pascale Patris, objects conservator; Marceline McKee and Suzanne L. Shenton, in the Loans Office; and Gary Burnett, Rob Davis, Sean Farrell, and Don E. Templeton, technicians in the American Wing.

We also wish to single out those members of the AFA staff whose efforts have been vital to the realization of this project: Thomas Padon, director of exhibitions; Donna Gustafson, chief curator; Kathryn Haw, curator of exhibitions; Michaelyn Mitchell, head of publications; Brian Boucher, interim head of education; Lisbeth Mark, director of communications; Kathleen Flynn, head registrar; Mary Grace Wahl, registrar; Beth Huseman, editorial assistant; Amy Poll, exhibitions assistant; and Stephanie Ruggiero, communications associate.

Thanks are owed to the designer and editor of this handsome catalogue, Eileen Boxer and Fronia W. Simpson, respectively.

Finally, we acknowledge with thanks the institutions that are presenting the exhibition: the San Diego Museum of Art; the Delaware Art Museum, Wilmington, Delaware; the Cheekwood Museum of Art, Nashville, Tennessee; the Orlando Museum of Art; and the New York State Museum at Albany.

PHILIPPE DE MONTEBELLO
Director, The Metropolitan Museum of Art

SERENA RATTAZZI
Director, American Federation of Arts

Acknowledgments

Many people have enabled us not only to organize this exhibition and to prepare this catalogue, but to have enjoyed doing so. At The Metropolitan Museum of Art, Philippe de Montebello, director, and Mahrukh Tarapor, associate director for exhibitions, supported our desire to share our collection of American Impressionist paintings by organizing an exhibition with the American Federation of Arts. Marceline McKee and Suzanne L. Shenton of the Loans Office handled innumerable administrative details with care and good judgment. Dorothy Mahon, paintings conservator, and Pascale Patris, objects conservator, offered their advice and ensured that the paintings and their frames were ready for travel. Dana Pilson and Catherine Scandalis, administrative assistants in the Department of American Paintings and Sculpture, helped to prepare the manuscript of the catalogue and to complete the loan forms, and aided us in other ways too numerous to count. The scholar Mary Munford Catlett handled additional details with respect to the publication and loans. Deanna D. Cross in the Photo and Slide Library arranged new photography for the catalogue. American Wing technicians Gary Burnett, Rob Davis, Sean Farrell, and Don E. Templeton provided invaluable help, as always.

At the American Federation of Arts, the energy and enthusiasm of Serena Rattazzi, director, initiated, encouraged, and invigorated the project. Her colleagues Thomas Padon, director of exhibitions, Donna Gustafson, chief curator, Kathryn Haw, curator of exhibitions, and Michaelyn Mitchell, head of publications, were crucial to our organizing the exhibition and preparing this publication. Their associates, Brian Boucher, interim head of education, Lisbeth Mark, director of communications, Kathleen Flynn, head registrar, Mary Grace Wahl, registrar, and Beth Huseman, editorial assistant, are also to be acknowledged.

We wish to thank Fronia W. Simpson for her tactful and intelligent editing of the text and Eileen Boxer for her handsome design.

We extend special appreciation to Richard York and Susan Menconi of the Richard York Gallery, who patiently offered advice.

Our research builds on the work of numerous colleagues. While most of them are acknowledged in the notes and bibliography, those mechanisms are inadequate to express our debt to Doreen Bolger, author of volume III of *American Paintings in The Metropolitan Museum of Art,* in which many of the works in this exhibition were catalogued for the first time. The entries on Mary Cassatt in volume II of the *American Paintings* catalogue, by Natalie Spassky, were also helpful. We are further indebted to the staff members, interns, fellows, volunteers, and student researchers in the Department of American Paintings and Sculpture, who, over the course of many years, have made the artists' files a mine of information. While most of their contributions have been anonymous, we would like to thank N. Mishoe Brennecke, Laurene Buckley, Gina M. D'Angelo, Arlene K. Nichols, Ashley Jacinth Thomas, and Catherine Hoover Voorsanger.

The staff of the Watson Library, especially Katria Czerwoniak (retired), formerly head of interlibrary loans, expedited the gathering of new information. Others at the Metropolitan Museum who aided our research include Stephanie L. Herdrich, Department of American Paintings and Sculpture; Jeanie M. James, Archives; Emily Martin, Costume Institute; and Elizabeth Milleker, Department of Greek and Roman Art.

Colleagues at other institutions, art dealers, independent scholars, relatives of the artists, and experts in other fields generously shared their knowledge. We deeply appreciate information on artists and paintings in the exhibition received from Ellen Adams; Dennis Anderson, The New York State Executive Mansion; Julie Aronson, Cincinnati Art Museum; M. Elizabeth Boone, Humboldt State University; Hildegard Cummings, Connecticut Artists Project; Georgiana Druchyk, Copley Society of Boston; Elizabeth Ellis, Museum of the City of New York; Thomas C. Folk; Susan Fraser, The New York Botanical Garden; Dr. Lee Ellen Griffiths, Monmouth County Historical Association; Dr. Gary D. Hermalyn, The Bronx County Historical Society; Nancy Allyn Jarzombek, Vose Galleries; Katherine Kaplan, Kraushaar Galleries; Matthew Kennedy; Kathleen Burnside Kilbride, Hirschl & Adler Galleries, Inc.; Elaine Kilmurray, John Singer Sargent catalogue raisonné; Leftwich D. Kimbrough; Allynne H. Lange, Hudson River Maritime Museum; Marguerite Lavin, Museum of the City of New York; Kathleen A. McAuley, The Bronx County Historical Society; Sandra H. Olsen, Castellani Art Museum, Niagara University, Niagara Falls; Melissa Orme; Robert McDonald Parker; Ronald G. Pisano; Lee Reich; Ruth Ridgeway, municipal historian, Windham, Connecticut; Marc Simpson; William Tarbell; and Carla Tobias, Monmouth County Historical Association.

H. BARBARA WEINBERG AND SUSAN G. LARKIN

Introduction

H. Barbara Weinberg

THE DEVELOPMENT OF AMERICAN IMPRESSIONISM

European Art in America, American Artists in Europe, 1860–1900

As the United States gained unprecedented international political and economic status after the Civil War (1861–65), American art patrons—notably Northerners who had made fortunes from the war—traveled abroad and absorbed European culture.[1] To announce their wealth and new sophistication, they built houses that rivaled European mansions and filled them with European art, especially canvases by old masters, French academics, and artists who painted at Barbizon.[2] In an effort to make their works attractive to prospective patrons, aspiring American architects, painters, and sculptors went to Europe to study. The ensuing internationalism of American art was not only a response to collectors' high regard for foreign styles and American artists' wish to emulate them, but reflected the presumption that the United States was entitled, and even obliged, to acquire, assimilate, and adapt the best the world had to offer.

Some American students of painting were attracted to Munich, but more often they flocked to Paris. Beautified under the Second Empire, the French capital had become the world's artistic center, noted for government-sponsored exhibitions, spirited critical debate, and newly professionalized art schools.[3] Whether at the Ecole des Beaux-Arts (the French government academy), or in private institutions, most students absorbed academic principles. They drew and painted the nude human figure, the key exercise, and learned anatomy, perspective, technical finesse leading to high finish, and the principles guiding lucid narrative exposition. Their goal was to portray complex figural subjects inspired by such timeless ideals as Truth and Beauty, literary and historical texts, exotic locales, or contemporary events; portraits, genre scenes, landscapes, and still lifes ranked lower in the subject hierarchy. Their ultimate mentors were artists who espoused the classical canon, starting with the Greek sculptors themselves, and moving on to Raphael, Nicolas Poussin, and Jacques-Louis David. Their actual teachers were students of David's students, or they painted as if they had been.

Art students who were attracted to pastoral imagery were inspired by the poetic canvases of the painters of Barbizon who had gathered since the early 1830s in the village on the edge of the Forest of Fontainebleau, about thirty-five miles south of Paris. At Barbizon, Jean-François Millet, a specialist in peasant genre, and landscapists such as Théodore Rousseau and Camille Corot sketched outdoors. Although these artists completed their paintings in the studio, they anticipated in their procedures and their ordinary subjects the French Impressionists' interest in working *en plein air* and capturing common experience.

The Training of the American Impressionists

American Impressionism matured toward the end of the period when American taste and art were transformed by contemporary foreign influences; it reached its apogee during the 1890s and was a mainstream style by the turn of the century. The practitioners included European-born artists such as John Singer Sargent (1856–1925); expatriates such as Mary Cassatt (1844–1926) and Frederick Carl Frieseke (1874–1939); frequent visitors to Europe such as William Merritt Chase (1849–1916) and Theodore Robinson (1852–1896); and relative stay-at-homes such as Edward Willis Redfield (1869–1965). Although it is difficult to make generalizations about the American Impressionists—they led varied professional lives and belonged to several generations— they were indisputably among the most thoroughly schooled, widely traveled, cosmopolitan painters in the history of our nation's art.

Most of the American Impressionists learned their early lessons in American academies that had been formed, or reformed, according to contemporary European standards with teachers who had studied abroad just after the Civil War. Almost all of them then went to Paris for further study. Some enrolled in the Ecole des Beaux-Arts, which was open, tuition-free, to men of any nationality. There they exercised either or both of two options: they applied to the *chef d'atelier* of one of the three relatively autonomous painting studios for admission to his class; or they passed the rigorous semiannual *concours des places* and matriculated in the school proper. In both divisions of the Ecole, draftsmanship was emphasized: by the *chef d'atelier* who expected a student to prove his competence in life drawing before allowing him to paint; and by the professor who oversaw daily life-drawing exercises in the matriculants' special class.

The American Impressionist J. Alden Weir (1852–1919), for example, studied first with his father, who was the drawing instructor at the United States Military Academy at West Point. He then worked from 1870 to 1872 at the National Academy of Design, New York, under Lemuel E. Wilmarth, a former student of Jean-Léon Gérôme, the most popular studio director among American pupils at the Ecole. When Weir went to Paris in 1873, he enrolled in Gérôme's studio and spent four years there; he also matriculated in the Ecole for three semesters between the fall of 1874 and the spring of 1877. Cassatt, who had begun intermittent studies in 1860 at the Pennsylvania Academy of the Fine Arts, Philadelphia, received private criticism from Gérôme about 1866—an unusual privilege for a woman art student—but her principal instructor in Paris was the painter Charles Chaplin, who conducted a special class for women. (A peripatetic student, Cassatt also worked in the French countryside—with Edouard Frère, Paul Soyer, and Thomas Couture—and in Italy.)

Other future American Impressionists in Paris entered new academies that competed with the Ecole des Beaux-Arts. These schools were privately owned, charged tuition, and expanded as their owners served aspiring students arriving from all over the world. The entrepreneurs simply rented more studios and hired more professors, the alter egos of those at the Ecole. The independent academies were a crucial resource for women, who were barred from the government school until 1897, and for other students who could not enter the Ecole or who preferred more flexible, if more costly, arrangements for instruction.

The Académie Julian, founded in 1868, was the most successful independent school and the usual Parisian training ground for the American Impressionists. Frank W. Benson (1862–1951), for example, had studied from about 1880 to 1883 at the School of the Museum of Fine Arts, Boston, before going to work at Julian's under Gustave-Rodolphe Boulanger and Jules-Joseph Lefebvre from 1883 to 1885. His friend Edmund C. Tarbell (1862–1938) followed the same pattern but remained at Julian's a year longer. Willard Metcalf (1858–1925) had attended several

Boston art schools, including the Massachusetts Normal Art School, the Lowell Institute, and the Museum School; he studied at Julian's under Boulanger and Lefebvre in 1883–84. Childe Hassam (1859–1935) had taken instruction from various Boston artists, had worked as an illustrator, and was more widely traveled than Benson, Tarbell, or Metcalf when he went to Paris to enroll at Julian's under Lefebvre, Boulanger, and Henri-Lucien Doucet from 1886 to 1889. Salon catalogues of 1887 and 1890 identify Robinson as a student of Jean-Joseph Benjamin-Constant, who taught with Jean-Paul Laurens at Julian's. Of the other artists represented in the current exhibition, Charles H. Davis (1856–1933), Ruger Donoho (1857–1916), Frieseke, Philip L. Hale (1865–1931), Louis Kronberg (1872–1965), Ernest Lawson (1873–1939), Arthur Frank Mathews (1860–1945), Redfield, John H. Twachtman (1853–1902), and Robert Vonnoh (1858–1933) also studied at Julian's, as did hundreds of other Americans.

Some students in Paris enrolled in more than one academy, as did Colin Campbell Cooper (1856–1937), who worked at Julian's and the Académie Délécluse, and Maurice Prendergast (1859–1924) and Walter Elmer Schofield (1867–1944), who worked at Julian's and the Académie Colarossi. Others entered studios organized by individual teachers. Sargent, for example, studied with the anti-academic portraitist Charles-Emile-Auguste Durand (who called himself Carolus-Duran) from 1874 until about 1879, and was indoctrinated by him into the Spanish Baroque painterly style rather than French Classicism. Sargent also visited the teaching atelier of Léon Bonnat, another portraitist influenced by Spanish art, and matriculated for three semesters of drawing instruction in the Ecole between the fall of 1874 and the spring of 1877.

Robinson sought out a range of influences. He had studied at the National Academy of Design in 1874–75 under Wilmarth and was evidently involved in the founding of New York's Art Students League, which also imparted academic principles. Between 1876 and 1879 Robinson worked in Paris under Carolus-Duran and in the Beaux Arts studios of Henri Lehmann and Gérôme, and he also matriculated in the Ecole for four semesters between the spring of 1876 and the spring of 1878. During the late 1870s he painted at Grez-sur-Loing, near Barbizon, and Veules-les-Roses, near Dieppe, and in Venice, where he met the American expatriate James McNeill Whistler. Robinson went back to the United States in 1879, settled in New York in 1881, and supported himself in part with mural painting and other decorative work. In May 1883 Robinson voiced the prevailing American cosmopolitanism in a letter to Kenyon Cox, a friend and fellow student at Gérôme's, noting: "I have nearly got rid of the desire to do 'American things'—mostly because American life is so unpaintable—and a higher kind of art seems to me to exclude the questions of nationality. I would like to try a little flight into something Biblical or Mythological."[4] Given the nature of Robinson's instruction, his internationalist aspirations are not surprising. In 1884 Robinson returned to France, where he would pass most of each year, spending the winters in New York. He may have studied with Benjamin-Constant at Julian's before he became a mainstay of the artists' colony that surrounded Claude Monet at Giverny in 1888.

Of the American Impressionists who were attracted to Munich, Chase was the most important. After receiving some art lessons in Indianapolis and working from 1869 to 1871 at the National Academy of Design under Wilmarth, Chase continued his studies abroad in 1872. He later explained: "I went to Munich instead of Paris because I could saw wood in Munich, instead of frittering in the Latin merry-go-round."[5] At least as important as Chase's schooling in Munich was the influence of Wilhelm Leibl, the German friend and alter ego of the French Realist

Gustave Courbet. To create his images of mundane subjects and familiar people, Leibl emulated the styles of Peter Paul Rubens, Frans Hals, and Rembrandt, using flashy brushwork and dramatic chiaroscuro. These traits, at odds with the academic emphasis on drawing and the classical canon, became the foundation of Chase's early paintings.

Some artists who had studied in Munich ultimately gravitated to Paris, enrolling, as did Twachtman, under Boulanger and Lefebvre at Julian's. Few American art students limited their experience of Europe to work in one city or even two. Most of them painted in the countryside around Munich or Paris and traveled to visit museums and picturesque sites, especially in Italy, Holland, and Spain. And most would have felt that their European studies were incomplete unless they submitted a canvas to an important competitive exhibition such as the annual Paris Salon, had it accepted by the jury, and seen it well displayed.

American Painters and Patrons Encounter French Impressionism

The French Impressionists made their debut in a private group exhibition in Paris in April 1874; they would show together until 1886, eight times in all. Their radical pictures challenged the rules that most American art students had learned at home and looked to have reinforced abroad. A rebuke to the academic emphasis on universal themes and meticulous technique were the Impressionists' beliefs that the artist's personal experience of modern life was the only viable source for subjects, and that mundane scenes should be rendered en plein air in unconventional compositions that enlisted rapid and broken brushwork and a high-keyed palette that would simulate the effects of light.

Impressionism attracted little notice from American art students in Paris, including the future American Impressionists, many of whom were there during its heyday. The French Impressionists' exhibitions held near the Opéra on the Right Bank were distant from the academies situated in the Latin Quarter on the Left Bank or in Montmartre in the northern part of the city. And because many of the Americans had scraped together precious funds for limited foreign study,

FIGURE 1
John Singer Sargent, *Oyster Gatherers of Cancale*, 1878. Oil on canvas, 31⅛ × 48½ inches. The Corcoran Gallery of Art, Washington, D.C.; Museum Purchase, Gallery Fund

FIGURE 2
John Singer Sargent, *In the Luxembourg Gardens*,
1879. Oil on canvas, 25⅞ × 36⅜ inches. Philadelphia
Museum of Art; John G. Johnson Collection

they would have followed their teachers' advice to visit the Louvre and Luxembourg museums and
not waste time with works by dissidents. Academic acolytes, the Americans would have scorned
the Impressionists' paintings, if they had seen them at all. Weir, then a student of Gérôme's, was
repelled when he visited the third Impressionist exhibition in the spring of 1877. He wrote home:
"I saw a show of a new school which call themselves 'Impressionalists.' I never in my life saw
more horrible things. . . . They do not observe drawing nor form but give you an impression of
what they call nature. It was worse than the Chamber of Horrors."[6] Weir was unusual among
the Americans in having recorded his reaction to the French Impressionists' works, but it was
undoubtedly typical.

Exceptions to the rule, Cassatt and Sargent caught the spirit of the new French painting during
the 1870s. Whereas most of the future American Impressionists intended to return to the United
States after studying abroad, Cassatt had chosen to settle in Paris in June 1874, just after she
turned thirty, and her parents and her sister joined her there in 1877. Sargent, only eighteen years
old when he arrived in Paris with his family in May 1874, seems never to have envisioned a residence other than Europe. That neither of the two artists had a family in the United States waiting
eagerly for reports of conventional successes may have helped them to put aside the expected for
the experimental.

A portrait that Cassatt showed in the 1874 Salon attracted the notice of Edgar Degas, who,
in 1877, invited her to exhibit with the Impressionists. Cassatt did so four times between 1879
and 1886 and helped to organize their displays. Her paintings, prints, and drawings in pastel
reveal her strong sympathies with their candid accounts of everyday experience, bold compositions, and spirited execution. Specifically she served as an empathetic but unsentimental witness to
the lives of women at a time when traditional gender roles were being transformed. By the 1890s
Cassatt was committed to her signature theme, mothers or nurses with children. About 1900 she
made a specialty of portraying children alone, as in *Portrait of a Young Girl* (1899; no. 37) and

FIGURE 3
William Merritt Chase, *Prospect Park, Brooklyn,*
ca. 1886. Oil on canvas, 17⅜ × 22⅜ inches.
Colby College Museum of Art, Waterville, Maine;
Gift of Miss Adeline F. and Miss Caroline R. Wing

Spring: Margot Standing in a Garden (Fillette dans un jardin) (1900; no. 36). She found an eager market for her distinctive images of nurturing women and their young charges.

By 1878 Sargent was nearing the end of his studies and was becoming known as a painter of stylish portraits and lively subject pictures. Some of the latter, such as *Oyster Gatherers of Cancale* (fig. 1), suggest in their informal compositions, high-keyed palette, and bravura brushwork the influence of Monet, whom Sargent seems to have met at the second Impressionist exhibition in 1876. Other canvases by Sargent, including vignettes of Third Republic Paris such as *In the Luxembourg Gardens* (fig. 2), echo images of commonplace urban incidents by Degas, Monet, Edouard Manet, Pierre-Auguste Renoir, and Gustave Caillebotte. While portraiture preoccupied Sargent increasingly during the early 1880s, subject pictures would always refresh his work, keep him in touch with people, places, and atmosphere beyond the studio, and help him to seize the suggestion of a specific moment.

Following the *succès de scandale* of his *Madame X (Madame Pierre Gautreau)* (1883–84; The Metropolitan Museum of Art, New York) in the 1884 Salon, Sargent decided to move from Paris to London. With time and creative energy to spare as he sought English patrons, he worked outdoors in the summers of 1885 and 1886 in the Cotswolds village of Broadway. His Impressionist efforts there were fostered by his continued contact with Monet, to whom he made several visits at Giverny, beginning in early summer 1885. At Broadway Sargent painted plein-air landscapes such as *Reapers Resting in a Wheat Field* (1885; no. 8), which captures with animated brushwork the rural spirit and golden sunlight that attracted visitors to the Cotswolds. Sargent spent portions of the summers of 1887, 1888, and 1889, respectively, in Henley, Calcot Mill, and Fladbury, England, where he also worked outdoors. Perhaps because he was removed from the distractions of the Broadway colony's social life and did not have a major exhibition piece underway,[7] he painted more canvases in the Impressionist vein, including *Two Girls on a Lawn* (ca. 1889; no. 32).

During the late 1870s other American painters gradually became aware of French Impressionism, partly as a result of increasing opportunities to see the French works in exhibitions in the United States and growing enthusiasm on the part of American collectors and critics. In 1877 Louisine Elder, later Mrs. H. O. Havemeyer, purchased a pastel by Degas with Cassatt's advice and in 1878 lent it to the annual exhibition of the American Water Color Society in New York. In 1879 an overview of French Impressionism in *Lippincott's Magazine* described the movement for American readers but criticized what it considered the bizarre palette and sketchiness of many paintings. In the winter of 1879–80 Manet's *Execution of the Emperor Maximilian* (1868–69; Städtische Kunsthalle, Mannheim) was shown in New York and Boston, and the painter was cited for his alliance with Emile Zola and literary naturalism.[8]

Weir, apparently encouraged by Chase, helped the New York collector Erwin Davis acquire Manet's *Boy with a Sword* (1861) and *Woman with a Parrot* (1866) in 1881; Davis gave both paintings to The Metropolitan Museum of Art in 1889. During the 1880s several large displays stimulated American interest in French Impressionism. In 1883 the Foreign Exhibition Association brought to Boston a show assembled by the French Impressionists' foremost dealer, Paul Durand-Ruel, which featured canvases by Monet, Renoir, Camille Pissarro, Alfred Sisley, and others. At the end of the same year, Chase guided the selection of paintings for the Pedestal Fund Art Loan Exhibition in New York, a show that included Davis's two Manets and a bold ballet scene by Degas.[9] In 1886 Durand-Ruel exhibited 290 paintings and pastels at New York's American Art Association. The dozens of works by each of the leading French Impressionists provoked extensive commentary in the press. Sales from the show, which was expanded and moved to the National Academy of Design, proved that American collectors were appreciative of radical art. Durand-Ruel gave Americans more opportunities to purchase pictures by opening a New York gallery in 1888 and mounting monographic exhibitions of the principal French Impressionists. The precocious patrons—Davis, the Havemeyers, and Alexander Cassatt, the painter's brother—were joined by others; their support and critics' growing attention to the movement would encourage more American painters to explore Impressionism.

Soon after Chase brought French Impressionist works to New York, he became the first major American artist to paint Impressionist canvases in the United States. This he did as early as 1886 in views of Central and Prospect parks in New York. Chase's freely brushed, light-filled park scenes such as *Prospect Park, Brooklyn* (fig. 3) took viewers to familiar places that were objects of national and municipal pride and were ideal analogues of the modern Parisian sites that Manet, Degas, Sargent, and others had painted. New York's handsome new parks were also outdoor counterparts of one of Chase's favorite subjects, his aesthetically arranged studio, and were similarly filled with artful accumulations of eye-pleasing elements.

Chase was more likely than his Paris-trained colleagues to have become an Impressionist without a struggle. Detached from academic prejudices and attracted to dissidents such as Leibl and Manet, he had been susceptible to a range of modern ideas. In 1881, for example, he met the Belgian painter Alfred Stevens, who had gained international patronage for his stylish blend of genre painting and portraiture. At Stevens's urging, Chase began to abandon the manner of Rubens, Hals, and Rembrandt that he had emulated in Munich under Leibl's influence and to adopt a more contemporary approach. In 1881 Chase also met Sargent and may have admired *In the Luxembourg Gardens*, which was conspicuous in New York during the mid-1880s.[10]

Whistler, whom Chase visited during the summer of 1885, was another likely influence. The famous expatriate had a long-standing interest in urban imagery, apparent in his French and English etchings of about 1860 and in his pastels of Venice, which stimulated Chase's experiments in pastel during the mid-1880s. Between 1872 and 1877 Whistler had painted park scenes featuring the milling crowds in Cremorne Gardens, London. Chase would have known of the infamous canvas from that series, *Nocturne in Black and Gold, the Falling Rocket* (fig. 4), which had provoked the Whistler-Ruskin libel suit in 1878.

Although Chase was exposed to French Impressionism indirectly, possibly through Sargent's works, and directly at New York exhibitions, his park scenes precede the major infusion of French Impressionist influence that affected American painters during the late 1880s and the 1890s. They are, thus, set somewhat apart from American Impressionism in general. Rather than pertaining only to French Impressionism, Chase's park paintings may be said to reflect an international interest in portraying modern life in a vigorous style that captured its dynamism and fragmentation, an interest of which French Impressionism was only one—albeit the most convincing and influential—manifestation.[11]

By the later 1880s American painters in France began to show increased appreciation of the Impressionists' candid images of modern life as engaging alternatives to the idealized subjects and refined technique that academic painters prescribed. Hassam, for example, adopted the Impressionists' palette and procedures for views of Paris, often tempering the radical style with some measure of academic control. Perhaps because Hassam had already painted Boston streetscapes under the influence of conservative urban painters such as Giuseppe de Nittis,[12] he was sympathetic to the Impressionists' city scenes. Moreover, because he sought French instruction only after he had matured as a painter, he may have been relatively resistant to academic strictures and open to the new painting. Hassam, along with Robinson and others who encountered French Impressionism in France, would transmit the style to his compatriots back in the United States.

The Attraction of Artists' Colonies Abroad

During the years when they studied in Europe, some of the future American Impressionists worked in artists' colonies. The popularity of these communities reflected the fading authority of academic subjects and the growing interest in commonplace themes. Liberating themselves from history painting, artists sought new experiences to sustain their endeavors and attempted to record them freshly and, more and more often, out-of-doors. The places and people they encountered in the countryside reflected what they thought to be simpler times and offered them and their patrons an antidote to—or at least a distraction from—the pressures and problems of industrial growth and urban life. Working in colonies, artists enjoyed contact with each other, the exchange of ideas, inexpensive accommodations, picturesque scenery, and local types who were accustomed to their presence and willing to serve as models.[13]

By the late 1880s several American painters had been drawn to Giverny, first by the charm of the village itself, forty miles northwest of Paris, and then by the presence of Monet, who had moved there from Vétheuil in May 1883. In the ensuing decades the French Impressionist master and his adopted village attracted painters from all over the world, of whom the Americans came in the greatest number. Metcalf may have been the first, arriving in the summer of 1885, about the time that Sargent apparently also visited Monet. In the same year, Robinson made his initial trip to Giverny, where he would return with several American friends to paint in the summer of 1887 and where he would spend long periods between 1888 and 1892. Cassatt's visit to Monet in October 1892 is mentioned in Robinson's diary.[14] A later generation of American Impressionists at Giverny included William de Leftwich Dodge (1867–1935), who spent the first of three summers there in 1898, and the expatriate Frieseke.[15] Not only was the "conversion" of many American painters to Impressionism stimulated and reinforced by their experience in Giverny, but the village's art colony would serve as a model for emulation when they moved elsewhere in Europe or returned to the United States.

Robinson's paintings of Giverny, such as *The Old Mill (Vieux moulin)* (ca. 1892; no. 9), reveal a dual academic-Impressionist manner. Apparently reluctant to renounce his lessons and dissolve forms in corrosive light, the artist articulated individual volumes before applying to them a chromatic veneer of broken strokes.[16] Influenced by Monet's growing interest in portraying French icons such as the façade of Rouen cathedral, grain stacks, and poplar trees, in canvases painted in series,[17] Robinson recorded Giverny's characteristic yellow stucco walls and red tile rooftops in multiple views. He thus seems to have laid the foundation for the several series of nationally resonant subjects that he painted after his final return to the United States in 1892.

While the artists' colony at Giverny nourished American Impressionism, other colonies in France also attracted American painting students, some of whom became Impressionists. Barbizon, the earliest large European artists' colony, appealed to painters of many nationalities well into the 1870s, when foreigners there began to outnumber their French colleagues. Even if younger artists could not work in personal contact with Millet or Corot (both of whom died in 1875), they were inspired by the aura of Barbizon.[18] Among many American artist-visitors was Charles H. Davis, who had seen Barbizon landscapes in Boston in the mid-1870s and had gone to Barbizon during the early 1880s. Robinson painted in Barbizon from time to time in 1884. Grez-sur-Loing, where artists had gathered intermittently since the 1830s, became an outpost for British and American painters who found there the same picturesque attractions that Barbizon offered, but with water—the river Loing. American devotees of Grez included Metcalf, Robinson, and Vonnoh.[19]

The principal expatriates among the American Impressionists were also involved in art colonies and other exurban venues. Cassatt's interest in landscape painting was limited, but during the summers she spent with her family in various rented houses not far from Paris, she was moved to paint women and children in gardens. After Cassatt acquired Beaufresne, a château in Mesnil-Théribus, fifty miles northwest of Paris, in the spring of 1894, she responded to the natural environment by using landscape settings for many paintings and pastels.

As has been noted, Broadway and other English villages stimulated Sargent's Impressionist experiments during the 1880s. After 1890, his long-standing wanderlust grew and he spent much time making travel studies on holidays or in connection with mural commissions. Sargent often visited Spain, Italy—especially Venice—and the Middle East, locales that nurtured his passion for recording color and light and impelled his unceasing production of oil sketches, watercolors, and more ambitious works. In *Alpine Pool* (ca. 1907; no. 13), for example, painted in the Val d'Aosta region of northwestern Italy, Sargent captured the appearance of forms submerged in sparkling water. Travel studies would become a new source of critical and financial support as he took on fewer portrait commissions.

Frieseke was the leader of a circle of American artists that came to be known as the Giverny Group after an eponymous exhibition held in New York in December 1910. Frieseke had first visited Giverny in the summer of 1905 and returned there for long summers and more extended periods thereafter until 1919, while also keeping a studio in Paris. In Giverny, Frieseke increasingly devoted himself to outdoor scenes. To render sunlight effects, he adopted more broken brushwork and a more vibrant palette than he had theretofore employed. He frequently turned to women in gardens as a subject. Frieseke's interest in gardens may have been provoked by Monet's devotion to portraying his own garden, but his keenest concern was the female figure, in emulation of Renoir. Thus, women in boudoirs, before mirrors, or passing the time reading, making music, or sewing engaged Frieseke's attention.

Activities of the American Impressionists in the United States

Most of the repatriated American Impressionists established themselves either in New York, where late-nineteenth-century American artistic activity was concentrated, or in Boston. New York's unprecedented cultural energy is reflected in Chase's professional life. He installed himself in a studio building at 51 West Tenth Street in Greenwich Village that had been constructed specifically for the use of artists. He exhibited with many new organizations, including the Society of American Artists, founded in 1877 to serve painters and sculptors who had studied in Europe and had discovered on their return that the National Academy of Design resisted cosmopolitan tendencies. Organizations such as the Society of Painters in Pastel, of which Chase was also a charter member, were created to serve American artists' interests in unfamiliar media, another defining trait of the period.

Chase devoted much time to teaching, becoming one of the most sought-after and successful American art instructors. He taught at the Art Students League almost every year between 1878 and 1896, and again between 1907 and 1912. During the 1890s he founded the Chase School (later called the New York School of Art and then the Parsons School), taught at the School of the Art Institute of Chicago, and began a twelve-year stint on the faculty of the Pennsylvania Academy of the Fine Arts. Between 1891 and 1902 he conducted summer classes in the Shinnecock Hills area of the town of Southampton, on Long Island's south fork; among his many students there were Annie Traquair Lang (1885–1918) and Gifford Beal (1879–1956).

Other American Impressionists benefited from the changes in the American art world that affected Chase. In addition to having new exhibition venues such as the Society of American Artists and the Society of Painters in Pastel, a group of American Impressionists showed together as Ten American Painters beginning in 1898; Chase would join this group in 1902, replacing Twachtman, who died that year. (Other artists in this exhibition who were members of the Ten include Hassam, Weir, Benson, Tarbell, and Metcalf.) Aside from Chase, Weir (1885–ca. 1897), Twachtman (1889–1902), and Metcalf (1891–92) taught at the Art Students League. Other art schools that employed American Impressionists were New York's Cooper Union, where Weir (1878–ca. 1897), Metcalf (1893–1903), and Twachtman (1894–1902) taught; the Pennsylvania Academy of the Fine Arts, where Vonnoh (1891–96; 1918–25) taught; and the School of the Museum of Fine Arts, Boston, where Vonnoh (1885–87), Tarbell (1889–1913), and Benson (1889–1917) offered instruction to younger artists, some of whom, such as F. Luis Mora, would work in an Impressionist vein.

American Impressionism stimulated and was served by summer art schools that featured open-air painting classes. Like Giverny in revolving around one artist was Shinnecock, which became a center for Impressionist studies under Chase's influence. Although Monet taught only informally and Chase was director of an art school, Shinnecock was in some ways an "American Giverny." Like the Norman village, it was both detached from and proximate to the main urban center, picturesque, and redolent of national foundations and earlier times. The Shinnecock Indians had sold the land that became the town of Southampton to English settlers (from Lynn, Massachusetts) in 1640. Southampton, including the Shinnecock Hills, was thus the oldest English settlement in New York State and matched the Massachusetts Bay Colony in climate, architecture, and general aspect.

The experiences of Chase and his students at Shinnecock were echoed in other colonies established by repatriated American painters, especially along the Atlantic coast near New York or Boston. These areas provided the essential inexpensive accommodations and picturesque subjects that these artists had enjoyed or observed in European colonies in addition to a strong sense of place. In New England (or New England–like) locales, American fundamentals—particularly associations with the period of settlement and colonial growth—were apparent and invited the repatriation of the American artistic spirit.[20] Impressionism was a foreign style, but it was inherently useful to cosmopolitan American artists who wished to express the essence of home.

The Cos Cob section of Greenwich, about thirty miles from New York City, and Old Lyme at the mouth of the Connecticut River, about ninety miles farther to the east, were notable Connecticut centers for the practice of American Impressionism. Both locales reiterated conditions that had prevailed in Giverny, including hospitable quarters in which some artists resided and others congregated: the Holley family's boardinghouse at Cos Cob, and Florence Griswold's house at Old Lyme. Twachtman settled in Greenwich in 1889 and soon began teaching at Cos Cob. Around him gathered Weir, Robinson, and Hassam, all of whom would work as Impressionists during the 1890s and impart their approach to younger associates such as Ernest Lawson and Allen Tucker (1866–1939).[21] Hassam and Metcalf were active at Old Lyme, a colony that would be identified with the academization of American Impressionism about 1900 and with a struggle between adherents of that style (as it became increasingly *retardataire*) and partisans of the even more old-fashioned Barbizon manner.[22]

East Hampton, New York, was dubbed the "American Barbizon" in an article in *Lippincott's Magazine* in 1883, to be cherished for its picturesque dwellings and old farmers and fishermen.[23] Donoho moved to East Hampton in 1891. Hassam found inspiration there beginning in 1907 and divided his time between New York and the Long Island village during the 1920s and 1930s. The area around New Hope in Bucks County, Pennsylvania, similarly picturesque and nostalgic, fostered an important colony of Impressionists in which Redfield and Schofield were key figures.[24]

Other areas to which the American Impressionists retreated individually or in groups of two or three—Chester, Vermont, in the case of Metcalf; Branchville, Connecticut, in the case of Weir; the Isles of Shoals in the case of Hassam—seem to have been chosen because, like the artists' colonies, they recalled aspects of nature and culture that the painters had experienced abroad and were at the same time redolent of the American spirit. Some American Impressionists based themselves and taught in other remote spots, as did Davis during summers beginning about 1892 in Mystic, on the Connecticut coast halfway between New York and Boston, and Robinson in 1893 in Napanoch, in New York's Catskill mountains.

Most of the repatriated American Impressionists took advantage of travel made easier by steamboat to make frequent trips to Europe to attend the regular exhibitions at London's Royal Academy of Arts and the Paris Salons; to gather inspiration in museums and galleries; to paint Impressionist works in picturesque places; or to spend seasons in artists' colonies, as did Robinson (in Giverny) and Vonnoh (who resided between 1907 and 1911 alternately in New York and Grez-sur-Loing). Chase was particularly peripatetic; he made many summer trips abroad during the 1880s and 1890s and taught summer classes in and around various European cities between 1896 and 1914. Canvases in the current exhibition that were created by repatriated American Impressionists during visits to Europe are Hassam's *July Fourteenth, Rue Daunou, 1910* (1910; no. 2) and Vonnoh's *Bridge at Grez* (ca. 1907–11; no. 11).

AMERICAN IMPRESSIONIST PAINTINGS IN CULTURAL CONTEXT

In general, American painters' adoption of Impressionism was delayed until the late 1880s, when the style had lost its radical edge in Europe and was validated by American collectors and critics. Yet that adoption was inevitable, given the pattern of American interest in French art and the material and cultural energy of the United States, which amplified the changes in modern life that had provoked and nurtured Impressionism in France. Those epochal changes included the shift from rural/agrarian to urban/industrial society; economic volatility, great disparities of wealth, and labor unrest; redefinition of the class structure and gender roles; growth and redistribution of population as a result of immigration and, in America, emancipation; and scientific challenges to religious beliefs.

It may at first appear that the American Impressionists, perhaps motivated by commercial concerns, merely imitated the surfaces of Impressionist paintings to compete with Monet and his colleagues for collectors' attention. Having been immersed in older French styles, they may have simply moved on from the academic or Barbizon manner to Impressionism, just as potential patrons had begun to build more up-to-date collections. While some American painters responded to Impressionism only superficially, the most interesting of them grasped its essence, especially the conviction that their works should encode modern life in modern artistic terms.

The Impressionists' insistence on familiar subjects provided a welcome antidote to the saturation of American painting by European academic and Barbizon influences, which favored universal figural themes and poetic, placeless landscapes, respectively. By the end of the 1880s, artists, critics, patrons, and other observers who had advocated internationalism in art and had asserted that American life was unpaintable—as Robinson had in May 1883—feared that "American" art had disappeared. Possibly in response to this anxiety, the repatriated American Impressionists sought genuine counterparts of French Impressionist subjects, sites that had local or national resonance or that announced American progress. The painters' conspicuous stylistic cautiousness, a vestige of their academic training, may even have been reinforced by their wish to be true to the subjects they depicted.

Since the early 1980s some scholars of French Impressionism have underscored the meanings of French Impressionist subjects, revising long-standing formalist notions that Monet and his contemporaries responded to motifs only as visual stimuli.[25] With these scholars' help, we appreciate the reciprocal relationship between the sites that the French Impressionists painted in and around Second Empire and Third Republic Paris and the new style in which they painted them. We interpret Monet's images of grain stacks, for example, as celebrations of French agricultural abundance, and his renderings of the façade of Rouen cathedral as emblems of national pride. French Impressionist paintings appear to be saturated with meaning as well as with light and color; they express not only the appearance but also the spirit of place.

Even more cosmopolitan than their French Impressionist counterparts, the American Impressionists experienced many places abroad and at home that energized their art. It is reasonable to assume that their paintings, like those of Monet and his colleagues, reflected their immersion in distinctive sites and their encounters with people of consequence to their private and professional lives, and to interpret them accordingly. For example, between 1896 and 1918 Hassam spent summers in Newport, Old Lyme, Cos Cob, Provincetown, and Gloucester, often depicting the colonial- and federal-period churches that were landmarks in these New England towns. While the churches that Hassam painted could be (and have been) viewed simply as convenient substitutes for Rouen cathedral and his many images of them described only in formal terms, it is at least as likely that Hassam intended to create icons of American religious freedom and tranquil tradition, signifiers—at a time of heightened patriotic sensitivity—of the nation in which his family's Yankee roots were deeply planted. If Monet's portrayals of Rouen cathedral invite and sustain symbolic readings, so do Hassam's paintings of New England churches.

The canvases included in this exhibition are arranged in thematic groups to suggest some of the ways in which the American Impressionists abroad and at home—and at home abroad—responded to aspects of the city and suburbs, the countryside, their artistic environments, and the domestic scene. Some of the paintings bridge thematic divisions or refer to more than one sort of experience. Like other American Impressionist works, these canvases bear witness to a dynamic period that invited artistic responses in a vibrant new style while they delight our eyes.

American Impressionists in the City and Suburbs

The American Impressionists abroad and at home witnessed the emergence from an agrarian tradition of an industrialized urban society. They were excited by the prospect of change and nostalgic for the rural past, enthusiastic about modern life and regretful that the reassuring and familiar were being swept away. Ignoring such problems as immigration and urban poverty, they shone a positive light on their era and chose to "concern themselves with the more smiling aspects of life, which are the more American," as William Dean Howells recommended writers do in *Criticism and Fiction* in 1891.[26]

Although the American Impressionists preferred to escape vexatious urban pressures, some were captivated by busy city streets. Satisfied with the rapidly rendered vignette rather than the artfully staged panorama, they could respond nimbly to the bustling spirit and the fragmented experience that marked the age. Hassam, who asserted that the artist who would claim lasting fame is he "who paints his own time and the scenes of every-day life around him,"[27] caught the flavor of characteristic neighborhoods in New York and Paris at engaging moments. In *Broadway and 42nd Street* (1902; no. 1), the area now known as Times Square—Manhattan's then new theater district—comes alive on a winter evening with twinkling electric lights, bustling crowds, and cabs and trolleys. The setting of *July Fourteenth, Rue Daunou, 1910* (1910; no. 2) is a fashionable street in the heart of the elegant district near the Paris Opéra, decorated for Bastille Day with flags of several nations.

Cooper made New York his specialty in works such as the atmospheric *Grand Central Station* (1909; no. 3). The painting actually offers a nostalgic record of a modern site that had already changed by the time Cooper painted it. The immense glass train shed that stood behind the Beaux Arts style railroad station on Forty-second Street and the steam-powered trains that Cooper depicted had disappeared, replaced by less intrusive—and less picturesque—structures and equipment.

The American Impressionists portrayed the edges of the cities and suburbs whose very creation encoded the shift from rural to urban existence that defined the period. They also painted resorts in which urbanites like themselves escaped unpleasant realities of city life. Lawson recorded the northern reaches of Manhattan in many canvases, especially prosaic activities along the Harlem and Hudson rivers near his residence in Washington Heights. In *The Bronx River* (ca. 1910; no. 4) he emphasized remnants of rural beauty still visible along a river whose banks were already transformed by industry. Beal, who lived in Newburgh, New York, about seventy miles north of New York City, captured scenes on the Hudson, including—as in *The Albany Boat* (1915; no. 5)—the crowds who took excursion boats to visit sites along the river. Although Prendergast painted glimpses of Boston, Venice, and New York early in his career, canvases that he executed after he settled in New York in 1914 are topographically ambiguous. While his *Group of Figures* (ca. 1918–23; no. 6), for example, may have originated as a scene in a seaside park, it evolved into an arcadian tapestry that reflects Impressionism and other modernist influences but resists simple stylistic categorization and identification of locale.

A familiar tourist destination was the subject of Hale's *Niagara Falls* (no. 7), painted on his honeymoon in 1902. Hale's image discloses its early-twentieth-century origins in the artist's emphasis on industry and technology: the new and graceful Upper Steel Arch Bridge, the tailraces of the mills that lined the river, and the Niagara Falls Power Plant. But, with an American Impressionist's typical euphemism, Hale presents these intrusions as harmonious additions to the natural panorama.

American Impressionists in the Countryside

In the countryside, the American Impressionists favored popular retreats that became artists' colonies. Scenes painted in European colonies suggest their preference for old-fashioned activities and nostalgic settings. Sargent's *Reapers Resting in a Wheat Field* (1885; no. 8) records farming near Broadway, the Cotswolds village whose vestiges of fast-fading rural traditions refreshed the spirit of painters and other urbanites. Robinson painted *The Old Mill (Vieux moulin)* (ca. 1892; no. 9) at Giverny as part of a series on a single subject that paralleled Monet's concurrent works in series. Like Sargent, Robinson focused on traditional agricultural elements: an old stone gristmill that converted into flour the grain that was grown on the distant hillside and gathered into grain stacks, forms that are also visible in the canvas.

Although Hassam was attracted to modern urban subjects, he also was drawn to old-fashioned rural scenes. In the summers during his student years in Paris, he painted at a friend's estate in Villiers-le-Bel, a village about ten miles north of the city that had been home to the painter Thomas Couture (with whom Cassatt had worked from May 1868 to April 1869). In at least one canvas made during a visit to the village, *Peach Blossoms—Villiers-le-Bel* (ca. 1887–89; no. 10), Hassam recorded a twisted tree in an overgrown corner of an orchard, capturing its unkempt, rustic charm. Vonnoh's painting *The Bridge at Grez* (ca. 1907–11; no. 11) memorializes a monument from more tranquil times, a massive and much-depicted stone bridge over the Loing in the riverside village that also was noted for its pearly gray light and hazy atmosphere. Schofield, who had been Vonnoh's student at the Pennsylvania Academy, was similarly attracted to nostalgic rural subjects. He painted *Sand Dunes near Lelant, Cornwall, England* (1905; no. 12) while he was living in St. Ives, a fishing village that had welcomed a colony of landscape painters seeking picturesque and physically daunting surroundings in a poor and remote region.

Aside from making works in artists' colonies, the American Impressionists responded to scenery they encountered on their travels in Europe. Sargent's *Alpine Pool* (ca. 1907; no. 13), painted in northwestern Italy, is only one of many images that document the expatriate painter's durable wanderlust and his ability to transform a tiny bit of nature into an engaging picture.

The American Impressionists' attraction to a variety of distinctive rural locales in the United States is suggested by several canvases in the exhibition. As a respite from his usual work as a figurative and decorative artist in San Francisco, Mathews painted landscapes on the Monterey peninsula south of the city, creating emblematic California coastal views, as in *Afternoon Among the Cypress* (ca. 1905; no. 14). Davis took as his subject for *August* (ca. 1908; no. 15) and other works the typical rock-strewn Connecticut hillsides near Mystic, the seaside village in which he settled about 1892.

Also engaged with New England villages was Metcalf, who joined the artists' colonies at Old Lyme, Connecticut, and Cornish, New Hampshire, but who painted alone in and around Chester, Vermont, during the last five years of his life. Metcalf portrayed the craggy northeastern landscapes in all seasons, as in *Hillside Pastures* (1922; no. 16), an unprepossessing but characteristic scene enlivened by the region's vibrant autumnal palette. Certainly, seasons as well as sites were defining local traits, as the Pennsylvania Impressionists realized when they made a specialty of winter images. The long months dominated by monochromatic earth and sky, leafless trees, and patchy snow cover in the area around New Hope in Bucks County are suggested in Redfield's *Overlooking the Valley* (1911; no. 17), a view within walking distance of his home.

American Impressionists in Their Professional Environments

As did Redfield in *Overlooking the Valley,* the American Impressionists frequently portrayed places near their homes and studios, which were often situated in suburbs or the countryside. During the early 1890s, Weir painted in Windham, Connecticut, where his wife's family lived. Weir's *Connecticut Village* (after 1891; no. 18) is similar in spirit to works he did on his farm in Branchville, in western Connecticut. It suggests the intimate scale of the streets and old houses that were preserved in towns in the state's rural northeast corner and that were cherished by urban visitors. After Twachtman settled in a farmhouse on Horseneck Brook in Greenwich, Connecticut, in 1889, he made the small waterfall on the property the subject of many paintings. As in *Horseneck Falls* (ca. 1889–1900; no. 19), he usually invited the viewer to encounter just a bit of nature, catching at a particular moment the color and light inflected by changes in the stream, the season, and the time of day. Tucker studied with Weir and Twachtman in summer classes at Cos Cob, Connecticut, in 1892. The influence of their lessons is apparent in the younger artist's *Winter at Portland* (1907; no. 20), an intimate note on a corner of Portland, a large working farm owned by a friend and located near Tucker's own home in Monmouth County, New Jersey.

Donoho moved to East Hampton on Long Island's south fork in 1890 and built a house in the Colonial Revival style on the edge of the village in 1894. Hassam visited Donoho, lived on and subsequently bought part of his property, and inspired Donoho to create garden images such as *Windflowers* (1912; no. 21). These share the style and sense of place of many of Hassam's own garden scenes. Beal, influenced by his teacher, Chase, painted at his family's Newburgh estate, a private counterpart of the public parks that had attracted Chase. Beal made a garden party, or "May fair," at the estate the subject of *Mayfair* (1913; no. 22), a canvas that captures a carefree moment in elegant surroundings.

In *Mannikin in the Snow* (ca. 1891–93; no. 23) Sargent parodied the traditional artistic practice of creating an imaginary scene from ordinary elements rather than recording them candidly. He and his friend, the American expatriate Edwin Austin Abbey, were working in Fairford, England, on murals for the Boston Public Library. For a diversion, they set up a mannikin in the snow outside their studio as a subject to paint. Abbey turned the draped figure into a troubadour; Sargent painted only what he saw.

Despite the American Impressionists' devotion to candor, they were not immune to the appeal of studio contrivances for some works. In the atrium of the Greek Revival mansion that Dodge built in Setauket, Long Island, in 1906, he placed a sculpture of a nude female torso, one of many versions of the so-called Medici Aphrodite. In his painting *Venus in Atrium* (1908 or 1910; no. 24), Dodge harmonized the torso with the plants and patches of sunlight that surround it by emphasizing the marble's rosy tints. Emulating Degas, Kronberg made dancers a thematic specialty, often portraying ballerinas backstage. Typically, *The Pink Sash* (1913; no. 25) is based on the unguarded moments that Degas recorded. However, Kronberg seems to concoct an arrangement of a young dancer and her older chaperone as if they were still-life objects in a studio setting.

As in *Fruit* (ca. 1888; no. 26) by Weir and *Still Life: Vase of Peonies* (ca. 1925; no. 27) by Tarbell, American Impressionists painted fruit and flower pieces and still lifes of other familiar and humble objects, echoing the interests of their French Impressionist counterparts such as Manet and Renoir. Such subjects embodied the American and French Impressionists' allegiance to ordinary forms rendered in informal compositions and with great painterly freedom.

The American Impressionists' professional lives are reflected in their portraits of their students, teachers, and friends. However casual these portraits may appear, many of them record intentional professional self-inventions by the portraitists or their sitters. For example, Chase's image of the sculptor Bessie Potter (ca. 1895; no. 28) alludes to a well-known self-portrait by the French painter Elisabeth-Louise Vigée-Lebrun, reiterating a guise and a presumed art-historical affiliation that Potter's friend and future husband, Robert Vonnoh, had constructed for her. In her portrait of Chase (ca. 1910; no. 29), Lang emulated her mentor's style so well that the canvas was once believed to be a self-portrait by Chase. Arthur Clifton Goodwin (1864?–1929) registered his debt to Kronberg by executing an uncharacteristic figure painting, *Louis Kronberg in His Studio in Copley Hall* (ca. 1913; no. 30), and by showing himself reflected in the mirror on the back wall. He also signaled Kronberg's debt to Tarbell by having him paint a woman doing needlework, Tarbell's favorite subject. Prendergast's *Portrait of a Girl with Flowers* (ca. 1913; no. 31) depicts his friend Edith Lawrence King, an artist and teacher whose own watercolors were influenced by his. King's portrait bears the imprint of Prendergast's distinctive style, as did her actual work.

American Impressionists Paint Domestic Life

Aspects of domestic life, usually featuring women at ease and charming children—often members of the artists' own families—were common subjects for the American Impressionists. Sargent's *Two Girls on a Lawn* (ca. 1889; no. 32) probably portrays his sister Violet and a friend reclining on the grass at Fladbury Rectory, about ten miles from Broadway in Worcestershire. The figures are so freely rendered that they defy identification and serve instead as icons of leisurely summer life in a country retreat. Working principally in Giverny between 1900 and 1920, Frieseke made a specialty of painting women, elegantly dressed or nude, in sunny gardens or in tasteful parlors or boudoirs. His *Woman with a Mirror (Femme qui se mire)* (1911; no. 33) captures feminine beauty and self-absorption observed during an intimate moment in an interior decorated with foliate forms—a garden indoors.

Repatriated American Impressionists created works in a similar spirit. Tarbell's *Across the Room* (ca. 1899; no. 34) depicts a beautifully dressed woman reclining on a Sheraton-style sofa in an elegant parlor. Such images of idle women embodied the prevailing notion, articulated in *The Theory of the Leisure Class* (1899) by Thorstein Veblen, that a woman at leisure announced her husband's or father's wealth and status. Sometimes genteel women were shown crocheting, sewing, or knitting, handicrafts that denied the contemporaneous shift to factory work and machine manufacture by unleisured women. Although women at ease were frequent subjects of the Boston Impressionists, whose leader was Tarbell, other American Impressionists also painted them. In *For the Little One* (ca. 1896; no. 35), Chase showed his wife sewing in their summer house at Shinnecock. As did Tarbell in *Across the Room,* Chase included in his interior old American furniture, which suggests the traditional values that the artists and the women they portrayed preserved and incarnated in the face of unpredictable modern life.

Cassatt suggested youthful vulnerability in her *Portrait of a Young Girl* (1899; no. 37). The pensive model wears a stylish costume, but Cassatt proposes that she is a child of nature by raising the horizon line in the scene; limiting the suggestion of egress along the fragmentary garden path; echoing the curving forms of her costume in the shapes of the shrubbery; and having her hold a blade of grass to her lips. The freshness of the setting and the bloom of the model's youth are coequal. Cassatt used similar devices more overtly in *Spring: Margot Standing in a Garden (Fillette dans un jardin)* (1900; no. 36), an image of a child who often modeled for her. The shapes of the costume are again reiterated in nature, and the rounded forms of the child's flesh and the unified palette amplify the connection between sitter and setting.

Benson's *Children in Woods* (1905; no. 38) conveys a similar message of carefree communion between innocent children and hospitable nature. The artist portrays his three daughters in a sun-drenched clearing at their summer home on the island of North Haven, Maine. The girls are reading a story, but Benson underplays even the minimal exertion of that pastime by obscuring the book that captivates them. The coincidence between youth and nature is even more explicit in Mora's *Flowers of the Field* (1913; no. 39), which he painted at his country home in Gaylordsville, Connecticut. Mora, who had studied with Tarbell and Benson, suggests that the country girls whom he depicts and the wildflowers they are arranging are equally innocent and delightful flowers of the field.

In the essays that follow, Susan Larkin traces in greater depth and detail the relationship of each of the paintings in the exhibition to the career of its creator and to its general cultural context. She is particularly attentive to how the artist's formal choices—composition, palette, and paint application, as well as the subjects depicted—provide clues to meanings. Both authors hope that the case studies presented here will stimulate consideration of other possible meanings for the works included in the exhibition. They hope, too, that American Impressionist canvases will come to be valued as suggestive and decipherable reflections of their creators' experiences abroad and at home, as well as enchanting records of light and color.

Notes

1. This essay reflects the methodology and some of the content of H. Barbara Weinberg, Doreen Bolger, and David Park Curry, *American Impressionism and Realism: The Painting of Modern Life, 1885–1915,* exhibition catalogue (New York: The Metropolitan Museum of Art, 1994). Some passages have appeared in H. Barbara Weinberg, *American Impressionism* (New York: Rizzoli International Publications, 1994).

2. The best account of the phenomenon appears in Edward Strahan [Earl Shinn], *The Art Treasures of America,* 3 vols. (Philadelphia: George Barrie, 1879–[82]; reprint, New York: Garland, 1977).

3. For American painters' pursuit of foreign training, see Michael Quick, *American Expatriate Painters of the Late Nineteenth Century,* exhibition catalogue (Dayton, Ohio: Dayton Art Institute, 1976); Lois Marie Fink, *American Art at the Nineteenth-Century Paris Salons* (New York: Cambridge University Press, 1990); and H. Barbara Weinberg, *The Lure of Paris: Nineteenth-Century American Painters and Their French Teachers* (New York: Abbeville Press, 1991).

4. Theodore Robinson to Kenyon Cox, Newport, R.I., May 31, 1883, Kenyon Cox Papers, Avery Architectural and Fine Arts Library, Columbia University, New York.

5. Quoted in Katherine Metcalf Roof, *The Life and Art of William Merritt Chase* (New York, 1917; reprint, New York: Hacker Art Books, 1975), pp. 30–31.

6. J. Alden Weir to his parents, Paris, April 15, 1877; quoted in Dorothy Weir Young, *The Life and Letters of J. Alden Weir* (New Haven, Conn.: Yale University Press, 1960; reprint, New York: Kennedy Graphics and DaCapo, 1971), p. 123.

7. Sargent had painted the ambitious *Carnation, Lily, Lily, Rose* (1885–86; Tate Britain, London) during his summers at Broadway.

8. See John Moran, "The American Water-Colour Society's Exhibition," *Art Journal* (New York) 4 (1878), p. 92; "The Old Cabinet," *Century* 15 (April 1878), pp. 888–89; L. Lejeune, "The Impressionist School of Painting," *Lippincott's Magazine* 24 (December 1879), pp. 720–27. All three articles are cited in William H. Gerdts, *American Impressionism* (New York: Abbeville Press, 1984), p. 49. See also "Manet and Zola," *Art Interchange* 3 (December 10, 1879), pp. 100–01.

9. For a detailed discussion of this exhibition, see Maureen C. O'Brien et al., *In Support of Liberty: European Paintings at the 1883 Pedestal Fund Art Loan Exhibition,* exhibition catalogue (Southampton, N.Y.: The Parrish Art Museum, 1986).

10. Sargent's park view had appeared in the 1879 sale of the John Sherwood collection in New York. It changed hands in 1884 and again in 1887, when it was sold at M. Knoedler and Company, New York, to John G. Johnson who would give it to the Philadelphia Museum of Art.

11. The concept of the simultaneous development of Impressionist styles in many countries is proposed in Norma Broude, ed., *World Impressionism* (New York: Harry N. Abrams, 1990). See especially pp. 28–34.

12. See Jennifer A. Martin Bienenstock, "Childe Hassam's Early Boston Cityscapes," *Arts Magazine* 55 (November 1980), pp. 168–71.

13. For a survey of the phenomenon of the artist community, see Michael Jacobs, *The Good and Simple Life: Artist Colonies in Europe and America,* exhibition catalogue (Oxford: Phaidon Press, 1985), and Steve Shipp, *American Art Colonies* (Westport, Conn.: Greenwood Press, 1996). For an introduction to the preoccupation with the peasant, see Gabriel P. Weisberg, *The Realist Tradition: French Painting and Drawing, 1830–1900,* exhibition catalogue (Cleveland: The Cleveland Museum of Art, in cooperation with Indiana University Press, 1980), and Richard R. Brettell and Caroline B. Brettell, *Painters and Peasants in the Nineteenth Century* (Geneva: Editions d'Art Albert Skira S.A., 1983).

14. Theodore Robinson diary, Cos Cob, Conn., October 3, 1892, Frick Art Reference Library, New York.

15. The best and most recent study of the American art colony in Giverny is William H. Gerdts, *Monet's Giverny: An Impressionist Colony* (New York: Abbeville Press, 1993). See also Laura L. Meixner, *An International Episode: Millet, Monet, and their North American Counterparts,* exhibition catalogue (Memphis, Tenn.: Dixon Gallery and Gardens, 1982).

16. The notion that the stylistic cautiousness of American Impressionism was rooted in its academic armature was first posited in H. Barbara Weinberg, "Robert Reid: Academic Impressionist," *Archives of American Art Journal* 15, no. 1 (1975), pp. 2–11, and developed in H. Barbara Weinberg, "American Impressionism in Cosmopolitan Context," *Arts Magazine* 55 (November 1980), pp. 160–65. The prior explanation of American Impressionist restraint as a vestige of the limner tradition can be found in Barbara Novak, *American Painting of the Nineteenth Century* (New York: Praeger Publishers, 1969), pp. 241–46.

17. See Paul Hayes Tucker, *Monet in the '90s: The Series Paintings,* exhibition catalogue (Boston: Museum of Fine Arts, in association with Yale University Press, 1989).

18. For a summary of the phenomenon, see Peter Bermingham, *American Art in the Barbizon Mood,* exhibition catalogue (Washington, D.C.: National Collection of Fine Arts, Smithsonian Institution, 1975), and Meixner, *An International Episode.*

19. See May Brawley Hill, *Grez Days: Robert Vonnoh in France,* exhibition catalogue (New York: Berry-Hill Galleries, 1987).

20. The late-nineteenth-century invention and uses of a reassuring image of New England is the subject of William H. Truettner and Roger B. Stein, eds., *Picturing Old New England: Image and Memory,* exhibition catalogue (Washington, D.C.: National Museum of American Art, 1999).

21. See Susan G. Larkin, "A Regular Rendezvous for Impressionists: The Cos Cob Art Colony, 1882–1920," Ph.D. diss., City University of New York, 1996, and Susan G. Larkin, *The Cos Cob Art Colony: Impressionists on the Connecticut Shore* (New Haven: National Academy of Design in association with Yale University Press, in press).

22. See Jeffrey W. Andersen, "The Art Colony at Old Lyme," in Harold G. Spencer, Susan G. Larkin, and Jeffrey W. Andersen, *Connecticut and American Impressionism,* exhibition catalogue (Storrs: University of Connecticut, 1980), and Jeffrey W. Andersen and Barbara J. MacAdam, *Old Lyme: An American Barbizon,* exhibition catalogue (Old Lyme, Conn.: Florence Griswold Museum, 1982).

23. Charles Burr Todd, "The American Barbison [sic]," *Lippincott's Magazine* 5 (April 1883), pp. 321–28. See *En Plein Air: The Art Colonies at East Hampton and Old Lyme, 1880–1930,* exhibition catalogue (Old Lyme, Conn.: Florence Griswold Museum; East Hampton, New York: Guild Hall Museum, 1989).

24. See Thomas C. Folk, *The Pennsylvania Impressionists* (Madison, N.J.: Fairleigh Dickinson University Press; London: Associated University Press, 1997).

25. See, for example, Theodore Reff, *Manet and Modern Paris,* exhibition catalogue (Washington, D.C.: National Gallery of Art, 1982); T[imothy] J. Clark, *The Painting of Modern Life: Paris in the Art of Manet and His Followers* (Princeton, N.J.: Princeton University Press, 1984); Robert L. Herbert, *Impressionism: Art, Leisure, and Parisian Society* (New Haven and London: Yale University Press, 1988); Tucker, *Monet in the '90s;* Richard R. Brettell, *The Impressionist and the City: Pissarro's Series Paintings,* exhibition catalogue (Dallas: Dallas Museum of Art, 1992); Anne Higonnet, *Berthe Morisot's Images of Women* (Cambridge, Mass.: Harvard University Press, 1992).

26. W[illiam] D[ean] Howells, *Criticism and Fiction* (New York: Harper and Brothers, 1891), p. 128.

27. Quoted in A. E. Ives, "Mr. Childe Hassam on Painting Street Scenes," *Art Amateur* 27 (October 1892), p. 116.

American Impressionists in the City and Suburbs

Broadway and 42nd Street, 1902

Oil on canvas, 26 × 22 inches
Bequest of Miss Adelaide Milton de Groot (1876–1967), 1967 (67.187.128)

"I believe the man who will go down to posterity is the man who paints his own time and the scenes of every-day life around him," Childe Hassam told an interviewer in 1892.[1] By that time, Hassam was already recognized as America's leading chronicler of modern life in the city. His gregarious personality predisposed him to this theme. "There is nothing so interesting to me as people," he declared. "I am never tired of observing them . . . as they hurry through the streets on business or saunter down the promenade on pleasure."[2]

Hassam demonstrated his fascination with the subject of the city in the watercolors he painted on his first trip to Europe, in the summer of 1883. Back in Boston the following year, he created his first important oils: views of stylish thoroughfares slicked with rain or covered with snow. When he returned to Paris in 1886 for a three-year stay, he again set up his easel in the streets. His preference for drizzly weather prompted one critic to urge him to "come in out of the rain."[3] By 1887, however, he was painting sun-drenched boulevards with the high-keyed palette and broken brushstroke associated with the French Impressionists.

Even after Hassam had become identified as an Impressionist, he retained a keen appreciation of the subtle atmospheric effects and unified palette favored by the Tonalists. In New York, where he settled permanently in late 1889, this persistent Tonalism was especially appropriate; he worked in the city mainly during the winter, withdrawing to the countryside from early summer to mid-autumn. In *Broadway and 42nd Street,* the predominantly blue-black palette conveys the city's glamour on a winter evening.

The crossroads that Hassam portrayed was, in the words of a contemporary observer, the "storm center of New York's hedonistic activities," especially at night, when it became "the glowing, incandescent heart of the city."[4] Now known as Times Square, when Hassam depicted it the area was still called Long Acre Square. That name linked New York's dynamic new theater district with the much older one in London (and is recalled today in the name of the Longacre Theatre). By 1902, the date of this painting, the streets around Broadway and Forty-second Street had only recently supplanted Union Square as the center of New York's commercial entertainment. The newly formed Metropolitan Opera Company initiated the shift uptown when it moved to its magnificent opera house on Broadway and Thirty-ninth Street in 1883. Five years later, the Broadway Theatre, which presented musical comedies and operettas, opened on Broadway and Forty-first Street. Between 1895 and 1900 the impresario Oscar Hammerstein built three theaters in Long Acre Square. So quickly did the neighborhood develop as a theatrical district that a contemporary of Hassam's could boast that Broadway's theaters "nightly suck in throngs of amusement seekers vaster than in any other of the world's thoroughfares."[5]

The glittering lights that punctuate Hassam's velvety dark image were so much identified with this district that it was dubbed "the Great White Way," a label that survives to the present day. Electric lights, which had been introduced to the neighborhood only seven years earlier, glow in the shop windows and in the trolley cars. Another signifier of modernity, the trolley system was, according to one commentator, "the greatest, as it is the newest, menace to the wayfarer on Broadway."[6] Hassam's Broadway blends new and old: the modern trolley cars with their brilliant electric lights run behind a row of horse-drawn cabs, whose paired lanterns accentuate the darkness.

Hassam probably set up his canvas in just such a cab to paint this picture. "I paint from cabs a good deal," he told an interviewer. "I paint from a cab window when I want to be on a level with the people in the street and wish to get comparatively near views of them, as you would see them if walking in the street."[7] His vantage point from the stationery cab plunges us into the action, re-creating the forced proximity with strangers that is typical of city life. Looming over the pedestrians, tall buildings bracket the composition on left and right. It is difficult to decipher any details that would aid in their identification, probably because Hassam believed that, seen individually, the new skyscrapers were "hideous." But "when silhouetted with a dozen or more other buildings against the sky," he maintained, they are "more beautiful than many of the old castles in Europe, especially if viewed in the early evening when just a few flickering lights are seen here and there and the city is a magical evocation of blended strength and mystery."[8]

Hassam's sunny daytime scenes of New York's parks and avenues reveal his debt to a slightly older generation of French artists; not only the Impressionists Claude Monet, Pierre-Auguste Renoir, Camille Pissarro, and Gustave Caillebotte, but also more academic painters like Giuseppe de Nittis and Jean Béraud. By contrast, the nocturnal *Broadway and 42nd Street* is more closely related to the work of his younger American colleagues, the urban realists often called the Ashcan school, who adopted similarly energetic brushwork and used black boldly. Yet, Hassam's work is more genteel than theirs. In contrast to the uninhibited shop girls and laborers depicted by Robert Henri, John Sloan, William Glackens, and George Luks, the elegantly dressed couple strolling toward the viewer in Hassam's oil is refined and discreet. Bridging Impressionism and Realism in *Broadway and 42nd Street,* Hassam revealed his continuing willingness to experiment.

1. A. E. Ives, "Mr. Childe Hassam on Painting Street Scenes," *Art Amateur* 27 (October 1892), p. 116.

2. Ibid., pp. 116–17.

3. *Boston Transcript,* 1887; quoted in William H. Gerdts, *American Impressionism* (New York: Abbeville Press, 1984), p. 97.

4. Richard Le Gallienne, "The Philospher Walks Up-Town," *Harper's Magazine* 123 (July 1911), p. 237.

5. John Corbin, "The Lights and the Stars of Broadway," *Scribner's Magazine* 37 (February 1905), p. 129. The information on the development of Times Square is from Mary C. Henderson, *The City and the Theatre* (Clifton, N.J.: James T. White & Co., 1973).

6. "Broadway by Night," *Harper's Weekly,* January 20, 1894, p. 54.

7. Ives, "Mr. Childe Hassam," p. 116.

8. Quoted in "New York the Beauty City," *New York Sun,* February 23, 1913, p. 16.

2 CHILDE HASSAM (1859–1935)

July Fourteenth, Rue Daunou, 1910, 1910
Oil on canvas, 29⅛ × 19⅞ inches
George A. Hearn Fund, 1929 (29.86)

To create this festive painting, Hassam positioned himself in the epicenter of French Impressionism. The site was just around the corner from the former studio of the photographer Félix Nadar, where the first Impressionist exhibition was held; the urban theme was identified with Edouard Manet, Claude Monet, Pierre-Auguste Renoir, and Camille Pissarro, and the high vantage point was one they had frequently employed for their views of Paris. Despite the fact that Hassam had often insisted that Impressionism stemmed from English roots, in *July Fourteenth, Rue Daunou, 1910* he paid a remarkable *hommage* to his French predecessors.

Because the title of Hassam's painting calls attention to a specific time and place, it is essential to understand what attracted him to this part of Paris on July 14, 1910. A short street connecting the boulevard des Capucines and the avenue de l'Opéra, rue Daunou was at the heart of the entertainment district—"le Paris des plaisirs," as a contemporary guidebook described it.[1] This fashionable neighborhood was markedly different from the bohemian artists' quarter where Hassam and his wife had lived more than twenty years earlier while he attended the Académie Julian. By 1910 Hassam was well established in his career and sufficiently prosperous to afford a prestigious location for a short holiday.

The Hassams stayed at the comfortable but not luxurious Hôtel de l'Empire, at number seven rue Daunou (the site is now occupied by the Théâtre Daunou). Using the hotel stationery, Hassam wrote to his friend J. Alden Weir on July 21, 1910, "I made a 14th July from the balcony here."[2] From his vantage point on the south side of the street, the artist looked down on the intersection of the rue Daunou and the famous rue de la Paix. In the distance is the boulevard des Capucines, where awnings shade the sidewalk cafés for which the lively thoroughfare was (and is) renowned.

Although rue Daunou was a relatively quiet side street, numerous stylish businesses filled its two-block length. Mrs. Hassam could choose among five hairdressers, four jewelers, a half-dozen lingerie shops, and at least eight dress boutiques. Five hotels, a florist, and several restaurants, bars, cafés, and *confiseries* (confectionery shops) served an upscale clientele, while a British realtor catered to English-speaking foreigners.

Hassam depicted the street decked with flags for the *fête nationale,* Bastille Day. On July 14, 1789, a furious crowd had stormed the Bastille, the fortress where political prisoners were incarcerated. The demolition of this hated symbol of despotism marked the beginning of the French Revolution; its anniversary commemorated the triumph of republicanism. Because the French national holiday followed the American one so closely, as the French Revolution had followed the American, contemporary accounts of the Bastille Day celebration often invoked the two countries' historical ties. For Hassam, the fourteenth of July would inevitably have recalled the fourth, suffusing his view of the French festivities with his ardent nationalism.

The artist expressed his patriotism by painting a plethora of American flags, which are outnumbered only by those of France. The repeated red, white, and blue of Old Glory and the French tricolor unify the composition, enlivening the buildings' dull masonry with cheerful accents. Furthermore, the shared national colors metaphorically suggest shared national values. Belgium's black, yellow, and red flag is also prominent, in honor of its monarchs, King Albert and Queen Elisabeth, then visiting Paris. Noting the numerous Belgian flags displayed in recognition of the royal visit, *Le Petit Journal* observed loyally that though they had the same design as the French, they were "of an appearance less joyful, of a color less vivid."[3] Scotland, England, and Ireland are each represented by one flag. The emerald banner of the Irish Independence Party echoes the foliage of a tree on the boulevard and the pale green shutters of the building in the right foreground.

While Hassam seems to have exaggerated the number of American flags decorating this corner of Paris, he was remarkably true to the specifics of time and weather. The overcast sky and motionless flags in his painting conform to the sultry, windless weather reported by the Paris newspapers. The minimal shadows suggest midday. Well-dressed men and women amble down the middle of the pavement, apparently unconcerned about the automobiles and horse-drawn conveyances. On this holiday, pedestrians had the right-of-way: vehicles were barred from the main boulevards and limited to a walking pace elsewhere.

The leisurely strollers whom Hassam observed from his hotel balcony could choose among a variety of amusements. Free afternoon performances were offered by three theaters in this district: the Vaudeville, the Athénée, and—just one block from Hassam's hotel—the Opéra. There, a production of *Aïda* attracted more than two thousand enthusiastic spectators, many of whom had begun lining up in the middle of the night.[4] Others in the street could wander the city listening to outdoor band concerts, playing carnival games, dancing on platforms at the major intersections, or buying pastries at sidewalk booths.

Hassam's view of Paris decked with flags had specific antecedents in the paintings of the French Impressionists and in his own work. Manet's *Rue Mosnier Decorated with Flags* (fig. 5) depicts the street near the French artist's studio. As Hassam would do almost three decades later, Manet employed a high vantage point, organized his composition around the plunging perspective of the street below, and showed an interest in the human element. But instead of filling his street with pleasure-seeking crowds, as Hassam

would do, Manet portrayed it as nearly deserted. A window-washer's ladder protruding from the lower edge of the canvas and a worker bending over a cart in the middle ground suggest the day-after letdown following the holiday, while the crippled man hobbling on crutches past a shabby fence represents the unglamorous realities ignored in the celebrations.[5]

Such mordant irony was foreign to Hassam, whose painting is more akin to Monet's *Rue Montorgueil, Festival of June 30, 1878* (1878; Musée d'Orsay, Paris). Monet's high-keyed canvas, which was exhibited in Paris in the early summer of 1889, may have inspired Hassam's first flag paintings: two watercolors and a small oil depicting Montmartre on Bastille Day.[6] But the American's most famous flag paintings are those he painted in New York City between 1916 and 1919.[7] In *Allies Day, May 1917* (1917; National Gallery of Art, Washington, D.C.), the patriotism that underlay *July Fourteenth* is wholeheartedly expressed, while the alliance with France—and Hassam's own emotional and artistic ties to that country—is honored in the bold blue, white, and red of the beleaguered nation's tricolor.

FIGURE 5
Edouard Manet, *Rue Mosnier Decorated with Flags,* 1878. Oil on canvas, 25¾ × 31¾ inches. J. Paul Getty Museum, Los Angeles

1. Paul Joanne, *Paris* (Paris: Librairie Hachette, 1913), p. 31.

2. Childe Hassam Papers, Archives of American Art, Smithsonian Institution, Washington, D.C., roll NAA-2.

3. "A Paris," *Le Petit Journal,* July 15, 1910, p. 2.

4. "Les Matinées gratuites," *Le Figaro,* July 15, 1910, p. 2; "Spectacles gratuits," *L'Intransigeant,* July 15, 1910, p. 2; and "A Paris," *Le Petit Journal,* July 15, 1910, p. 2.

5. See Robert L. Herbert, *Impressionism: Art, Leisure, and Parisian Society* (New Haven: Yale University Press, 1988), pp. 30–32, for a perceptive analysis of this painting.

6. The watercolor *Fourteenth July, Paris, Old Quarter* (1887–89) is in the Museum of Art, Carnegie Institute, Pittsburgh. The location of the watercolor *July Fourteenth, Montmartre, Paris* (1889) is unknown, as is that of the oil.

7. See Ilene Susan Fort, *The Flag Paintings of Childe Hassam,* exhibition catalogue (Los Angeles: Los Angeles County Museum of Art, 1988).

July Fourteenth, Rue Daunou (detail)

3 COLIN CAMPBELL COOPER (1856–1937)

Grand Central Station, 1909
Oil on canvas, 33 × 44¾ inches
Gift of the family of Colin Campbell Cooper, in memory of the artist and his wife, 1941 (41.22)

The Grand Central Station to which Cooper's title refers was constructed between 1869 and 1871 and enlarged, with the addition of three floors and a new stone-masonry façade on Forty-second Street, in 1899. Cooper eschewed a view of that imposing façade. In his cityscape, only the domed towers to the right and left of center suggest the building's impressive public face. Instead, the painter focused on the dark train shed overlooking the busy, smoky yards behind the station.

The train shed, fabricated of glass and wrought iron, "covered the largest interior space on this continent" and was, during its early years, "a sightseers' attraction second only to the Capitol in Washington," as a railroad historian has noted.[1] Tourists were awed by its vast interior, spanned by arches two hundred feet wide. They could admire its highly ornamental exterior curtain wall from one of the pedestrian bridges that crossed the station yard. From that vantage point, they could also marvel as the coal-fired, steam-powered locomotives moved into and out of the depot, accelerating until they went beneath street level north of the station at Park Avenue and Fifty-sixth Street.

By the time Cooper painted this canvas, conditions and attitudes had changed. As rail traffic increased dramatically—from eighty-eight trains every weekday when Grand Central Station opened in 1871 to three hundred at the end of the nineteenth century—the active tracks in the heart of the city were reviled as noisy, dirty, and dangerous. After fifteen people were killed in a collision in the Park Avenue tunnel in 1902, the New York State legislature decreed that by 1908 no coal-fired trains could enter the city south of the Harlem River.[2] Instead, within Manhattan, trains would be required to run on electrical energy. The shift to electricity permitted a dramatic change in midtown Manhattan and the elimination of the landscape Cooper recorded on this canvas. In a massive ten-year

construction project that began in 1903, the tracks were buried below street level and a tree-shaded boulevard was built up over the train yard, converting Park Avenue from a scruffy industrial artery to an elegant boulevard whose name is synonymous with urban chic.[3]

Cooper must have felt a sense of urgency when he first recorded this disappearing landscape in 1906 in *Old Grand Central Station* (Montclair Art Museum). Excavation and construction in the yard had by then been underway for three years. By 1909, when he painted the Metropolitan's *Grand Central Station*, the old train shed had been demolished and electric-powered trains were running out of a temporary station east of the old depot. The painting's most prominent elements were only a memory.

Cooper's continued engagement with a landscape that no longer existed was probably prompted by both nostalgia and an impulse to document the city's appearance at a time of rapid change. Furthermore, he seems to have retained the attitude toward steam that had prevailed decades earlier. In the last quarter of the nineteenth century, billowing steam was a literary and visual metaphor for progress and modernity. Three characters in William Dean Howells's novel *A Hazard of New Fortunes* (1890) admire a steam engine as they wait on an elevated-railway platform. "*Look* at that thing! Ain't it beautiful?" exclaims one. The others "leaned over the track and looked up at the next station, where the train, just starting, throbbed out the flame-shot steam into the white moonlight." The sight was, another observer declared, "the most beautiful thing in New York—the one always and certainly beautiful thing here."[4]

That attitude toward steam-powered trains is also evident in nineteenth-century paintings by J. M. W. Turner, George Inness, members of the Hudson River school, and the French Impressionists.[5] While most

of those images contrast the modern train with a rural landscape, Cooper's treatment of the theme echoes Claude Monet's series depicting the Gare St.-Lazare in Paris. Both Cooper's *Grand Central Station* and Monet's canvases show a smoky railroad yard in the heart of the city.

By the time he recorded this lost landscape of New York, Cooper was well known for his cityscapes. The son of a Philadelphia surgeon, he had begun his professional training at the Pennsylvania Academy of the Fine Arts, where Thomas Eakins was one of his teachers. He traveled in Europe in 1885, but it was not until after his marriage to fellow artist Emma Lampert in 1897 that he sought academic training there. He studied at the Julian and Délécluse academies in Paris and painted in Spain, the Low Countries, and the French provinces. On sketching holidays, he developed a penchant for architecture, painting châteaux and churches, courtyards and cloisters. He returned to Philadelphia in November 1901 but recrossed the Atlantic the following year to paint the cathedral towns of England.

On his return from England late in 1902, Cooper settled in New York and immediately began his long series of modern urban views. According to a contemporary critic, Cooper discovered in skyscrapers "a distinctive New World product . . . with which the Old World had nothing to compare. They had not the flavor of antiquity, but they had . . . the spirit of progress and promise, the manifestation of a surging, restless, all-attempting, all-achieving life essentially American."[6] Although Cooper's best-known works are devoted to those skyscrapers, some of his apparently modern urban scenes such as *Grand Central Station* reiterate the nostalgia that inflected his earlier views of historical European architecture. In 1921 he retired to Santa Barbara, California, where he was a leader in the artistic community until his death.

1. Carroll L. V. Meeks, *The Railroad Station: An Architectural History* (New Haven: Yale University Press, 1956), p. 86.

2. Deborah Nevins, "Grand Central: Architecture As a Celebration of Daily Life," in Deborah Nevins et al., *Grand Central Terminal: City Within the City* (New York: Municipal Art Society, 1982), p. 12.

3. Matthew Kennedy, "Reform Politics, Public Pressure, and the Beginnings of New York's Terminal City," in Renate L. Colella et al., eds., *Pratum Romanum: Richard Krautheimer zum 100. Geburtstag* (Wiesbaden: Dr. Ludwig Reichert, 1997), pp. 215–17. I am grateful to Mr. Kennedy for information on Grand Central.

4. William Dean Howells, *A Hazard of New Fortunes* (1890; New York: New American Library, 1965), p. 143.

5. See Leo Marx, "The Railroad-in-the-Landscape," in Susan Danly and Leo Marx, eds., *The Railroad in American Art: Representations of Technological Change* (Cambridge, Mass.: The MIT Press, 1988), pp. 183–208.

6. Willis E. Howe, "The Work of Colin C. Cooper, Artist," *Brush and Pencil* 18 (August 1906), pp. 76–77.

4 ERNEST LAWSON (1873–1939)

The Bronx River, ca. 1910

Oil on canvas, 21 × 25 inches
Gift of Mrs. J. Augustus Barnard, 1979 (1979.490.13)

The Bronx River flows from the hills of Westchester County south through the center of New York's northernmost borough. By the end of the nineteenth century, industrial buildings encroached on its banks except in Bronx Park, whose seven hundred acres encompass the New York Botanical Garden and the Bronx Zoo. The river meanders through the park, splashing down waterfalls and twisting through woodlands. For this painting, Lawson selected a transitional landscape, probably on the fringes of the park, where the evidence of light industry had not yet destroyed the natural beauty.[1]

Lawson's attraction to this semirural setting reveals the influence of his most revered teachers, John H. Twachtman and J. Alden Weir. Lawson, who was born in Canada, met Twachtman when he enrolled at the Art Students League in 1891. He followed Twachtman to Cos Cob, Connecticut, for his summer class in 1892, when Weir shared the instruction. Declaring one of Lawson's early landscapes the worst he had ever seen, Weir offered advice the nineteen year old would follow for the rest of his career: "Simplify everything and stick to your first impression . . . , for you can do no more than suggest things in nature."[2]

Lawson sailed for France in 1893. In Paris he enrolled at the Académie Julian, where Twachtman had studied a decade earlier. Holidays that Lawson spent painting in the French countryside offered him the opportunity to develop the skills he had learned in Cos Cob. A chance encounter with the painter Alfred Sisley at Moret-sur-Loing, a village near the Fontainebleau forest, strengthened the young American's commitment to Impressionism. Lawson later recalled Sisley's criticism: "All he said was, after looking over the canvas and then taking in my appearance, 'Put more paint on your canvas and less on yourself.'"[3]

When Lawson visited Cos Cob in the summer of 1894, Theodore Robinson saw some of the landscapes he had painted in France. "Not very personal—a little too much like a lot of other men," the astute Robinson noted in his diary[4]; Lawson had not yet found his distinctive subject or style. Lawson was well aware of the difficulties of reconciling diverse influences in an original way. After spending two more years in France, he confided his concerns in a letter to a cousin. "As far as influence goes, we can get too much," he wrote. "I want to keep my individuality and at the same time get as much of the best French influence as will be consistent with it. As with medicine French influence kills if taken in too large a dose—witness most of our best artists who have become to all intents and purposes Frenchmen in work and thought. Now I will go back again to Connecticut, and see what I can do."[5]

Lawson would be best able to demonstrate what he could do, not in the Connecticut countryside, but on the fringes of New York City. He settled on 155th Street in Washington Heights in 1898; for the next fifteen years, the surrounding landscape would be his major subject. Most of his canvases depict the prosaic, unlovely edges of the Harlem and Hudson rivers. A cluster of factory buildings, a shabby boathouse, a pigeon coop atop a laborer's cabin: such were the unremarkable subjects in which he detected some element of beauty. The Bronx River, however, shows him seeking an urban counterpart of Twachtman's Horseneck Brook. "Movement in nature is my creed as a landscapist and light and air are my delight," Lawson declared.[6] Here, he captured the sense of nature's constant motion in the play of light over the water and through the foliage. He selected a stretch of the river spanned by a nondescript bridge and punctuated by a functional mill, then juxtaposed the angular solidity of those industrial structures with the evanescent luminosity of their natural setting. The mill's peony pink reflection shimmers against the swirling dark green water in the "crushed-jewels" palette that critic James G. Huneker identified as characteristic of Lawson's best work.[7]

The period during which Lawson painted The Bronx River proved to be the peak of his career. He earned critical accolades and exhibited widely. Although he called himself a traditionalist, he participated in progressive artists' organizations, including the Eight. Like his colleague in the Eight, Maurice Prendergast, Lawson applied pigments in a thick tapestry of brushstrokes. He shared the Ashcan school's devotion to urban themes but avoided the social commentary with which they imbued their canvases. Instead, he reconciled an older style with newer subject matter, bridging Impressionism and Realism in a decorative Post-Impressionist style.

1. For their help in identifying the painting's site, I am grateful to Dr. Gary D. Hermalyn, executive director, and Kathleen A. McAuley, curator, The Bronx County Historical Society, and Susan Fraser, head, information services and archivist, The New York Botanical Garden.

2. Ernest Lawson, "The Credo," ca. 1930s; reprinted in Henry Berry-Hill and Sidney Berry-Hill, Ernest Lawson: American Impressionist (Leigh-on-Sea, England: F. Lewis, Publishers, 1968), p. 22.

3. Lawson, "The Credo," p. 22.

4. Theodore Robinson diary, Cos Cob, Conn., August 25, 1894, Frick Art Reference Library, New York.

5. Quoted in Barbara O'Neal, Ernest Lawson, 1873–1939, exhibition catalogue (Ottawa: National Gallery of Canada, 1967), p. 8.

6. Lawson, "The Credo," p. 22.

7. Quoted in F. Necolin Price, "Lawson, of the 'Crushed Jewels,'" International Studio 78 (February 1924), p. 367.

5 GIFFORD BEAL (1879–1956)

The Albany Boat, 1915
Oil on canvas, 36⅜ × 60¼ inches
George A. Hearn Fund, 1917 (17.48.1)

Steamboat travel on the Hudson River was a popular means of transportation and recreation from 1807 until 1971. Daytrippers enjoyed excursions with stops for sightseeing and picnics, while long-distance travelers appreciated the comfortable cabins of the night boats that plied the Hudson from New York City north to the Catskills. The closed superstructure of the vessel in *The Albany Boat* indicates that it was one of the boats that ran every night between lower Manhattan and the state capital. While not a completely accurate depiction of any one vessel, it resembles the *Kaaterskill,* which had berths for three hundred passengers.[1]

Newburgh, where Beal had a home overlooking the Hudson, was an important landing for the steamboats. (For Beal's biography, see number 22.) Day boats stopped to allow excursionists to visit George Washington's Revolutionary War headquarters; night boats stopped to take on passengers and freight. Beal delighted in observing the vessels and, as this painting reveals, their passengers. His large canvas is animated with amusing vignettes of human activity: three boys in striped sweaters ogle the crowd; a little girl in a white dress strides confidently ahead of her parents; a well-dressed woman pushing a baby buggy pauses to chat with friends; in the center, oblivious to all the bustle, a plump middle-aged man sprawls on a park bench reading a newspaper.

While the theme of middle-class leisure links Beal to the Impressionists, his sympathetic eye for varied human activity aligns him with the Realists. Like them, Beal often filled his canvases with more figures, of a wider range of social classes, than did the Impressionists. For example, in *For the Little One,* a painting in this exhibition by William Merritt Chase (no. 35), Beal's former teacher depicted a young mother sequestered in a refined interior. In *The Albany Boat,* by contrast, Beal portrayed women and children mingling with strangers in a crowded public space.

The vigorous brushwork of *The Albany Boat* also reflects the combined threads of Impressionism and Realism. Beal took to heart Chase's advice: "Never be sparing in the use of paint; always paint with a full brush."[2] Yet Beal's paint handling seems closer to that of such Realists as William Glackens and the Post-Impressionist Maurice Prendergast than to Chase's. *The Albany Boat* appears to have been quickly painted; single strokes define an arm or a torso, short cross-hatched strokes suggest the trampled grass, and thicker impasto describes the texture of the tall evergreen.

Beal painted several other views of Hudson River steamboats. At least two of them depict the famous day boat the *Mary Powell,* which was named for his great-grandmother.

---

1. I am grateful to Allynne H. Lange, curator of the Hudson River Maritime Museum, for information on the Hudson River steamboats.
2. Quoted in Gifford Beal, "Chase—the Teacher," *Scribner's Magazine* 61 (January 1917), p. 257.

6 MAURICE PRENDERGAST (1858–1924)

Group of Figures, ca. 1918–23

Oil on canvas, 23¼ × 27¾ inches
Bequest of Miss Adelaide Milton de Groot (1876–1967), 1967 (67.187.136)

Prendergast's anomalous position in American Impressionism can be grasped by comparing his *Group of Figures* with Childe Hassam's *July Fourteenth, Rue Daunou, 1910* (no. 2). Prendergast was one year older than Hassam, but his art has affinities with a newer style than that of his fellow Bostonian. Hassam's oil is informed by the cityscapes of Claude Monet, Pierre-Auguste Renoir, and Camille Pissarro. Prendergast's canvas, by contrast, is an arcadian vision more akin to the coloristic innovations of the Fauves, the decorative patterns of the Nabis, and the inscrutable meanings of the Symbolists. Like Paul Cézanne, who belonged to the same generation as the French Impressionists but whose style and influence are more closely related to the art of their successors, Prendergast straddles the fluid boundary between Impressionism and Post-Impressionism.

Prendergast was born in St. John's, Newfoundland. His father, who was Irish, was a merchant; his mother was the daughter of a Boston physician. After the father's business failed, the family moved to Boston in 1868. Prendergast left school when he was about fourteen to go to work. He apprenticed as a designer of advertising display cards while attending free evening drawing classes at the Starr King School in Boston.[1] His younger brother and fellow artist Charles later told an interviewer that Maurice "knew he wanted to be an artist right from the start, and he didn't let anything stand in his way."[2] His earliest extant works are a group of Barbizon-inspired watercolors he painted in Wales during a trip with Charles in the summer of 1886. Back in the United States, he began painting watercolors at New England beach resorts, concentrating on images of women and children at leisure.

In 1891, ready to make the transition from commercial designer to painter, Prendergast sailed for Paris, where he enrolled at the Académie Julian and Colarossi's studio. Having had little formal artistic training in the United States, he was less prepared for his French studies than most Americans, but more receptive to the most progressive work in the Paris exhibitions. He became part of an English-speaking international group that included the Canadian painter James Morrice and the English artist Charles Conder, who was part of Henri de Toulouse-Lautrec's circle. While still a student, Prendergast developed a sophisticated modern style influenced by such Post-Impressionists as Pierre Bonnard and Edouard Vuillard, the leaders of the group known as the Nabis.

Back in Boston between 1894 and 1898, Prendergast continued to paint children at play and women at leisure. He concentrated on making watercolors, which he sent to exhibitions in Boston, New York, Philadelphia, and Chicago. Critics responded warmly to his lyrical images, and his works sold well. He spent about eighteen months in 1898–99 in Italy, where he produced a suite of sparkling Venetian watercolors that sold readily to discriminating collectors on his return to Boston.

Prendergast had his first one-man show in New York at the Macbeth Gallery in 1900. From that time on, he developed a network of friendships with New York artists and spent part of every year painting the city's streets and parks. He began to work more in oils, applying the paint in thick layers of short strokes. A trip to France in 1907 reaffirmed his interest in the avant-garde movement. He was exhilarated by the expressive, brightly colored Fauve paintings of Henri Matisse, Georges Braque, Maurice de Vlaminck, and André Derain. "I am delighted with the younger Bohemian crowd, they outrage," he wrote to Charles after visiting the Salon d'Automne. "Even the Byzantine and our North American Indians with their brilliant colors would not be in the same class with them."[3] During that stay in Paris, Prendergast also saw two exhibitions of the work of Cézanne, who proved to be another important influence on his work.

Prendergast brought the new ideas home from Paris to his friends in Boston and New York. Diverging from the modern-life subjects of the American Impressionists and Realists, he recast motifs of middle-class leisure into timeless pastorales, using the devices of flattened space, tapestry-like brushwork, and stylized forms that he had admired in the works of the French modernists. Critics did not always understand his deliberately naïve paintings. After viewing the exhibition of the Eight at the Macbeth Gallery in 1908, one critic complained that "the canvasses of Maurice Prendergast look for all the world like an explosion in a color factory."[4]

Prendergast returned to Italy in 1911. He had prostate surgery in Venice and spent his convalescence poring over art books, especially those on Byzantine and pre-Renaissance Italian art. On his return to the United States early in 1912, he became involved in planning the Armory Show, the exhibition that in 1913 introduced modernist European art to a vast American audience. Even Prendergast was shocked by the paintings of Pablo Picasso and the other Cubists he saw there for the first time. Asked his opinion of the show, he remarked, "Too much—O my God!—art here."[5]

Prendergast moved to New York in 1914. From then until his death, he continued to keep up with emerging artists and trends. Although it never evolved into complete abstraction, his own work became increasingly arbitrary in color and stylized in composition. *Group of Figures,* for example, defies logical analysis. The central tree seems to grow through the bench; ghostly figures and fragmented bodies betray the artist's second thoughts; even his name, in the signature at lower right, is misspelled. (Nonetheless, the painting's authenticity is undisputed.) However, the sinuous outlines, vivid colors, and sense of well-being make this a representative example of Prendergast's late style.

1. Ellen Glavin, "The Early Art Education of Maurice Prendergast," *Archives of American Art Journal* 33, no. 1 (1993), pp. 4–5.
2. Hamilton Basso, "A Glimpse of Heaven—I," *New Yorker* 22 (July 27, 1946), p. 26.
3. Quoted in Nancy Mowll Mathews, *Maurice Prendergast,* exhibition catalogue (Williamstown, Mass.: Williams College Museum of Art, 1990), p. 24.
4. Ibid., p. 26.
5. Ibid., p. 29.

Niagara Falls, 1902

Oil on canvas, 25 × 30 inches
Gift of Rita and Daniel Fraad, Jr., 1978 (1978.509.4)

Philip Leslie Hale painted this unusual view of Niagara Falls on his honeymoon with fellow artist Lilian Westcott Hale. By the time they arrived soon after their wedding on June 11, 1902, the falls were already a cliché as a destination for newlyweds. "Every American bride is taken [to Niagara Falls]," the British wit Oscar Wilde had quipped twenty years earlier, "and the sight of the stupendous waterfall must be one of the earliest, if not the keenest, disappointments in American married life."[1] The Hales, however, were far from disappointed. Within a few days of their arrival, they wrote home to ask that their portable easels be shipped to Niagara so that they could stay on and paint.

Hale's letters reveal his search for fresh vantage points. Well aware that Niagara was an iconic theme in American art, he believed that only the Boston painter William Morris Hunt had succeeded in capturing the cascades' raw power.[2] He had high ambitions for his own attempts, confiding to his sister, the artist Ellen Day Hale, "we hope to paint things that will make all the former views of Niagara look like thirty cents."[3]

Hale completed several paintings of Niagara Falls. For two of them (Pfeil Collection, Chicago, and Vose Galleries, Boston), he depicted Horseshoe Falls with tourists strolling along the bank and the sightseeing boat, *Maid of the Mist,* near the base. For the Metropolitan's canvas, he ignored the familiar postcard views. He set his easel near Table Rock on the Canadian shore. Frederic Edwin Church had exploited that viewpoint for his famous *Niagara Falls* (1857; The Corcoran Gallery of Art, Washington, D.C.); a generation before Church, the preacher-painter Edward Hicks had depicted tiny human figures peering at the awesome cataract from Table Rock (fig. 6).[4] But Hale turned away from the panorama that he had traveled far to see. Instead of the magnificence of nature, he celebrated the wonders of technology. The focal point of his

composition is the graceful Upper Steel Arch Bridge. Completed just four years before Hale's visit, the bridge was by far the longest of its type in the world. Its 840-foot span, which offered stupendous views of the falls, carried the first trolley line that connected the United States and Canada. Modern and strong, yet as delicate visually as a garden trellis, the bridge was considered "one of the wonderful things to be seen at Niagara."[5]

In Hale's composition, the cascades spilling down the cliffs are the tailraces of the American pulp and flour mills that ran on power generated by the falls. In a possibly ironic reference to Niagara's fame as a honeymoon destination, one of those streams of wastewater was nicknamed Bridal Veil Falls.[6] Seen just beyond the mills in Hale's painting is the Niagara Falls Power Plant, which at its construction in 1890 represented the world's first major development of hydroelectric power.[7] The juxtaposition of natural grandeur and modern industry appealed to Hale. "[T]here are very interesting motifs of factory chimneys . . . with the falls behind," he wrote to his father, "I don't object to the two forces together—there is something elemental about both."[8]

Hale rendered this view of natural and industrial power in the Impressionist style he had developed in France. After studying at the School of the Museum of Fine Arts, Boston, under Edmund C. Tarbell and at the Art Students League, New York, under J. Alden Weir, he sailed for Paris in 1887. He would live there for five years, studying at both the Ecole des Beaux-Arts and the Académie Julian. His education as a landscape painter, however, came during the summers he spent in the rural Norman village of Giverny. There, as one of the first generation of American art colonists, he adopted the bright colors and spontaneous brushwork associated with the paintings of Giverny's most famous resident, Claude Monet. Hale's friendship with fellow

FIGURE 6
Edward Hicks, *The Falls of Niagara,* 1825. Oil on canvas, 31¼ × 38 inches. The Metropolitan Museum of Art; Gift of Edgar William and Bernice Chrysler Garbisch, 1962

artist Theodore Butler provided a link to the French master. He served as a witness at Butler's marriage to Monet's stepdaughter Suzanne Hoschedé in July 1892 and published a description of Monet's famous home and garden a few months later.[9] After Hale moved back to Boston, he maintained a correspondence with his friends in Giverny. Convinced that Monet could succeed at painting Niagara where others had failed, he planned "to write to Monsieur Monet and beg him to come over and try his hand."[10] In Hale's own highly individual rendition of the American landmark, Monet's influence is evident in the golden afternoon light, the high viewpoint, and the shimmering, silken hues of the broad river.

1. Oscar Wilde, "Impressions of America," 1883; quoted in Elizabeth McKinsey, *Niagara Falls: Icon of the American Sublime* (Cambridge: Cambridge University Press, 1985), p. 178.

2. Philip L. Hale to the Hale family, no date, Sophia Smith Collection, Smith College, Northampton, Mass.

3. Philip L. Hale to Ellen Day Hale, summer of 1902, Sophia Smith Collection.

4. McKinsey, *Niagra Falls*, pp. 46 and 244.

5. Orrin E. Dunlap, "The Romance of Niagara Bridges," *Strand Magazine* 18 (November 1899), p. 433.

6. For this and other information, I am grateful to Sandra H. Olsen, director of the Castellani Art Museum, Niagara University, Niagara Falls, New York.

7. Writers' Program of the Work Projects Administration, *New York: A Guide to the Empire State* (New York: Oxford University Press, 1940), p. 277.

8. Philip L. Hale to Edward Everett Hale, July 4, 1902, Sophia Smith Collection.

9. Philip L. Hale, "Our Paris Letter," *Arcadia* 1 (September 1892), p. 179.

10. Philip L. Hale to Ellen Day Hale, June 1902, Sophia Smith Collection.

American Impressionists in the Countryside

8 JOHN SINGER SARGENT (1856–1925)

Reapers Resting in a Wheat Field, 1885

Oil on canvas, 28 × 36 inches
Gift of Mrs. Francis Ormond, 1950 (50.130.14)

Sargent painted *Reapers Resting in a Wheat Field* at a turning point in his career. The expatriate artist, who was born in Florence to American parents, had enjoyed a peripatetic childhood abroad. In his youth, he became an accomplished pianist, mastered four languages, and demonstrated prodigious gifts for drawing and painting. He studied briefly at the Accademia delle Belle Arti in Florence before moving in 1874 to Paris. There he enrolled in the studio of the city's most celebrated portrait painter, Charles-Emile-Auguste Durand (Carolus-Duran) and in drawing classes at the Ecole des Beaux-Arts. Success came early to Sargent. He was only twenty-one when, in 1877, his first submission to the annual Salon was accepted. His Salon entry for the following year, *Oyster Gatherers of Cancale* (fig. 1, p. 14), was praised by critics; in 1879 his portrait of Carolus-Duran (Sterling and Francine Clark Art Institute, Williamstown, Mass.) earned him an honorable mention, accolades in the press, and a flurry of portrait commissions.

The ensuing years saw the steady mounting of Sargent's international renown—and the "uncanny spectacle," in Henry James's words, "of a talent which on the very threshold of its career has nothing more to learn."[1] Travels in Spain, Holland, Venice, and North Africa enabled Sargent to study the works of Diego Velázquez and Frans Hals and inspired the genre paintings he submitted to the Salons along with society portraits. The upward trajectory of Sargent's career was deflected in 1884, when his *Madame X* (1883–84; The Metropolitan Museum of Art, New York) outraged the sitter, her family, and many visitors to the Salon. Crowds gathered before Sargent's portrait of the famous beauty to mock her revealing décolletage,

lavender-toned makeup, and arrogant pose. Sargent's portrait commissions dwindled. He traveled to England in the summer of 1884 to fulfill commissions received months before the Salon fiasco. The following summer he returned, this time to enjoy a complete respite from the demands of formal portraiture.

Together with his fellow American expatriate the painter and illustrator Edwin Austin Abbey, Sargent retreated to the village of Broadway. Located in the rolling farmland of the Cotswolds, Broadway had become a popular artists' colony. The core members of the group were American expatriates—Sargent, Abbey, the painter Francis Davis Millet, and the novelist Henry James—who were attracted by Broadway's handsome old stone houses and the pastoral beauty of the landscape. The village and the surrounding Worcestershire countryside were, according to James, "the perfection of the old English rural tradition."[2] Broadway supplied a treasure trove of nostalgic detail for Abbey's and Millet's literary illustrations. "The garden walls, the mossy roofs, the open doorways and brown interiors, the old-fashioned flowers, the bushes in figures, the geese on the green, the patches, the jumbles, the glimpses, the color, the surface, the general complexion of things, have all a value, a reference and an application," James wrote, adding mischievously, "It is delicious to be at Broadway and . . . not to have to draw."[3]

Sargent lodged at the Lygon Arms, an old coaching inn, but spent most of his time across the green at Farnham House, which had been rented by the Millet family.[4] The British poet Edmund Gosse later recalled the fourteenth-century priory in the Millets' garden, where "Henry James and I would write, while Abbey

and Millet painted on the floor below, and Sargent and [the English painter Alfred] Parsons tilted their easels outside. We were all within shouting distance, and not much serious work was done, for we were in towering spirits and everything was food for laughter."[5] In the evenings, Sargent contributed to the entertainment by playing Wagner's complete *Ring* cycle. "We have music until the house won't stand it," Abbey reported to a friend.[6]

Surrounded by comrades, detached from the frustrations of his Paris career, and freed from the constraints of portraiture, Sargent enthusiastically took up plein-air painting. He had met Claude Monet at the second Impressionist exhibition in 1876 and their friendship developed through the years. In Broadway in the summer and autumn of 1885, Sargent was able for the first time to concentrate on painting in the open air, employing the high-keyed palette and concern with light characteristic of the Impressionists. During that sojourn, he began the major work, *Carnation, Lily, Lily, Rose* (1885–86; Tate Britain, London), depicting two girls in white dresses lighting Japanese lanterns in the garden at Farnham House. However charming and informal it appears, the painting is contrived; Sargent ordered cartloads of rosebushes from London, tied artificial flowers from his friends' hats onto bare shrubbery, and, in his determination to complete the painting the following year, had his shivering young models pose outdoors in drizzly November.

By contrast, *Reapers Resting in a Wheat Field* retains the spontaneity of a canvas painted on the spot in one or only a few sessions. Its theme of rural labor sets it apart from the upper-class leisure that inspired most of Sargent's Broadway canvases. Agricultural subjects were popular among British and European artists—and their urban, cosmopolitan patrons—in the last quarter of the nineteenth century. Contrasting approaches to the theme are represented by the influential French artists Jean-François Millet, who ennobled farmworkers,[7] and Jules Bastien-Lepage, who exposed their hardships. In his famous *Les Foins* (fig. 7), which attracted attention when it was exhibited at the Salon of 1878 and in London two years later, Bastien-Lepage depicted two downtrodden peasants at rest. Unlike Sargent, he revealed the sometimes dehumanizing rigors of farm work in the woman's open-mouthed stare and exhausted posture. Sargent, on the other hand, kept his distance from the farmers, depicting them not as individuals, but as essential and harmonious elements in the landscape.

Reapers Resting conveys the simple pleasures of a summer afternoon in the English countryside. The bright palette communicates the warmth of midday sun. The farmers' tools—the sickles—mimic the sickle-shaped brushstrokes Sargent adopted about this time. A network of short, curved strokes in tones of yellow, brown, violet, blue, green, and pink captures the glint of sunlight on the newly shorn wheat. This glorification of English country life links Sargent to John Constable and other eighteenth- and early-nineteenth-century painters, to poets such as William Wordsworth, and even to the designers of pastoral figurines in Chelsea and Bow porcelain.

FIGURE 7
Jules Bastien-Lepage, *Les Foins,* 1878.
Oil on canvas, 71 × 77 inches. Musée d'Orsay, Paris

1. Henry James, "John S. Sargent," *Harper's New Monthly Magazine* 75 (October 1887), p. 684; quoted by Marc Simpson in Marc Simpson with Richard Ormond and H. Barbara Weinberg, *Uncanny Spectacle: The Public Career of the Young John Singer Sargent,* exhibition catalogue (New Haven: Yale University Press, 1997), p. 31.

2. Henry James, *Picture and Text* (New York: Harper and Brothers, 1893), p. 4.

3. Ibid., p. 6.

4. Stanley Olson, "Sargent at Broadway," in Stanley Olson, Warren Adelson, and Richard Ormond, *Sargent at Broadway: The Impressionist Years,* exhibition catalogue (New York: Coe Kerr Gallery, 1986), p. 17 [and elsewhere].

5. Quoted in Richard Ormond, *John Singer Sargent: Paintings, Drawings, Watercolors* (New York: Harper & Row, 1970), p. 33.

6. Quoted in E. V. Lucas, *Edwin Austin Abbey; Royal Academician: The Record of His Life and Work* (New York: Charles Scribner's Sons, 1921), vol. 1, p. 152.

7. Sargent made several copies of Millet's etchings about 1875; four of them are in the Metropolitan's collection.

Reapers Resting in a Wheat Field (detail)

The Old Mill (Vieux moulin), ca. 1892

Oil on canvas, 18 × 21⅞ inches

Gift of Mrs. Robert W. Chambers, 1910 (10.2)

Theodore Robinson's ambivalence in responding to the relative claims of Americanism and cosmopolitanism was manifested in his choice of places to live and paint. For a time, it appeared as if he might follow the pattern of Sargent and Cassatt and become a permanent expatriate. Ultimately, however, his extended residence in France was followed by a final, and very fruitful, four years in the United States.

Robinson was born in Irasburg, Vermont, and grew up in Evansville, Wisconsin. He began his artistic education in 1870 at the Chicago Academy of Design, but after only a few months he was forced to return home to recuperate from the severe asthma that would shorten his life. In 1874 he went east to New York and enrolled at the School of the National Academy of Design. Two years later, he sailed for Paris to complete his training. Although three Impressionist exhibitions were held between 1876 and 1879, Robinson's student years in Paris, his work of that period reveals no trace of their influence. Instead, he emulated the methods of his teachers: the careful draftsmanship of the history painter Jean-Léon Gérôme and the fluid brushwork and restrained palette of the society portraitist Charles-Emile-Auguste Durand (Carolus-Duran). Both mentors were perennial stars of the yearly Salon exhibitions, and Robinson aspired to similar recognition. When, in 1877, one of his paintings was hung in the Salon for the first time, he wrote to his mother, "My picture is accepted and I tremble with joy."[1]

After returning to the United States in 1879, Robinson applied the skill in figure painting he had developed in the French studios to nostalgic images of rural life similar to those painted by Winslow Homer and Eastman Johnson. He soon rejected this subject matter and reported to a friend who had also studied under Gérôme, "I have nearly got rid of the desire to do 'American' things—mostly because American life is so unpaintable."[2]

By 1884 Robinson had saved enough money to return to Europe. For the next eight years, he would spend most of each year in France, usually returning to New York in the winter. He lived for a time in Barbizon, the village in the Forest of Fontainebleau made famous earlier in the century by the presence of the painters Jean-François Millet, Théodore Rousseau, and their circle. In their subdued tones and rustic themes Robinson's paintings of the mid-1880s reflect the influence of these Barbizon painters. His interest in Impressionism was growing, however, and in 1885 he was taken to visit Claude Monet at his home in Giverny by a mutual friend, the French painter Ferdinand Deconchy.[3] Two years later, Robinson and four friends spent the summer in Giverny, thus initiating the predominantly American art colony there. Robinson would live in Giverny for about half of each year from 1888 through November 1892.

Unlike most of the painters who would flock to that village over the next two decades, Robinson became a close friend of Monet's. The French artist's influence is apparent in Robinson's lightened palette, freer brushwork, interest in light effects, and tendency to treat the same subject in a series of canvases. But unlike Monet, Robinson took as his major theme the workaday life of Giverny's peasants.

Located in rural Normandy, Giverny is surrounded by rolling fields of wheat and oats. When Robinson lived there, the small village supported no fewer than three gristmills. Despite the painting's title, the mill that Robinson portrayed does not appear to be the one called the Vieux moulin (Old Mill), but rather the Moulin de Chennevières, which was built between the fourteenth and seventeenth centuries.[4] Robinson depicted the mill from the rear, with the country lane dropping from sight as it dips to the river Ru. On the opposite bank, on the same axis as the road, is a grain stack, whose newly harvested stalks would eventually be threshed and carried to the mill to be ground into flour. Beyond, plow-ridged fields rise to the horizon. Fields, grain stack, and mill summarize the seasonal cycles, from cultivation to harvest to milling.

About the time Robinson was painting the old mill, Monet was engaged in several of his ambitious series: of grain stacks (1890–91), poplars (1891), and Rouen cathedral (beginning in 1892). Emulating Monet's seriality, Robinson portrayed the mill at least five times. He depicted it glowing in the moonlight in two oils—Moonlight, Giverny (1892; The Parrish Art Museum, Southampton, N.Y.) and a study for the latter (Graham Williford Collection)—and a watercolor of the same scene (Mr. and Mrs. Raymond J. Horowitz). A daylight version is Road to the Mill (1892; Cincinnati Art Museum).[5] In that oil, which is slightly larger than the Metropolitan's, a young peasant woman herds a cow down the lane toward the viewer. Sunlight dances over the figures, the road, and the building, in contrast with the overcast sky and muted light in The Old Mill.

Just before Robinson left Giverny at the end of November 1892, he took photographs of "the little mill," apparently to help him continue work on the series in his New York studio. Back in his native land, he turned instead to characteristically American scenes. Despite this shift in subject, many of Robinson's American works—his series based on the disused Delaware and Hudson Canal at Napanoch, New York, and his views of the Palmer & Duff Shipyard at Cos Cob, Connecticut, for example—echo the nostalgic mood and the interest in oldtime industry that pervade his paintings of the mill at Giverny. Robinson never returned to France. He died in New York on April 2, 1896, at forty-four.

1. Quoted in Pearl H. Campbell, "Theodore Robinson: A Brief Historical Sketch," Brush and Pencil 4 (September 1899), p. 288.

2. Theodore Robinson to Kenyon Cox, Newport, R.I., May 31, 1883, Kenyon Cox Papers, Avery Architectural and Fine Arts Library, Columbia University, New York.

3. Pierre Toulgouat, "Skylights in Normandy," Holiday 4 (August 1948), p. 67.

4. I am grateful to Maureen Lefèvre, acting administrator, Musée d'Art Américain, Giverny, for identifying the site of the painting, faxes dated December 9, 1997, and July 29, 1998, in object file, Department of American Paintings and Sculpture, The Metropolitan Museum of Art.

5. William H. Gerdts lists these works as a series depicting the same building in his book Monet's Giverny: An Impressionist Colony (New York: Abbeville Press, 1993), p. 92. Gerdts identifies "a different Giverny mill," the Moulin de Chennevières, as the probable site of three additional oils by Robinson: Père Trognon and His Daughter at the Bridge (1891; Terra Foundation for the Arts, Chicago), The Watering Place (1891; Baltimore Museum of Art), and La Débâcle (1892; Scripps College, La Jolla, Calif.); see Gerdts, Monet's Giverny, p. 94. However, the small outbuilding next to the road in The Old Mill series appears identical to the structure in the background of the Père Trognon series. The current resident of the Moulin de Chennevières, who verifies that it is the subject of The Old Mill, identified the small structure as the caretaker's lodge in a conversation with me in June 1998.

10 CHILDE HASSAM (1859–1935)

Peach Blossoms—Villiers-le-Bel, ca. 1887–89

Oil on canvas, 18⅛ × 21½ inches
Gift of Mrs. J. Augustus Barnard, 1979 (1979.490.9)

This captivating view of a gnarled peach tree frothed with blossoms marks one of Childe Hassam's early forays into a theme that became a favorite: the garden. Painted in France, in a style influenced by Asian art, it also reflects the cosmopolitanism of an artist who, more than most, insisted on his undeviating Americanism.

Hassam was born in Dorchester, Massachusetts, into a family whose New England roots extended back to the seventeenth century. Despite his pride in his Yankee ancestry, he took perverse delight in having a surname, originally Horsham, that might be construed as Middle Eastern. To emphasize its exoticism, he dropped his first name, Frederick, and added a crescent moon to his signature, as in the inscription at the lower right of this painting. "Hassam," however, is pronounced in standard American fashion with the accent on the first syllable.

The artist's father had been a prosperous merchant and antiques collector before his business was destroyed in a fire that swept Boston in 1872. In the aftermath, the young Hassam was forced to leave high school, probably in 1877, and go to work. Over the next few years, he supported himself, first as a draftsman in a Boston wood-engraver's office and later as an illustrator, while attending classes in anatomy, drawing, and painting at the Lowell Institute and the Boston Art Club. Two of his teachers, the Italian Tommaso Juglaris and the German Ignaz Gaugengigl, introduced him to the dominant European strains prevalent in the instruction of late-nineteenth-century American artists. Juglaris had studied in Paris with Jean-Léon Gérôme and Alexandre Cabanel, while Gaugengigl represented the Munich academic tradition.

Hassam visited Europe for the first time in the summer of 1883, traveling to England, Scotland, Holland, France, Switzerland, Spain, and Italy. Back in Boston,

he continued working as an illustrator and spent much of his leisure time painting outdoors in the city and, less frequently, the country. In the city, he focused on the stylish and up-to-date, but in the country, he favored the rustic and old-fashioned. Influenced by the agrarian landscapes of the Barbizon painters, whose work had been popularized in Boston by Hassam's distant relative, the painter William Morris Hunt, the young artist depicted rutted farm lanes and humble barnyards.

In 1886 Hassam returned to Paris with his wife, the former Maude Doan, for a three-year stay intended to complete his artistic training. Like many Americans, he enrolled at the Académie Julian, where he studied under Jules-Joseph Lefebvre and Gustave-Rodolphe Boulanger. He soon grew bored with French academic methods, however, and resumed his practice of working on his own. His only opportunities to paint in the French countryside were on his visits to an estate about ten miles north of Paris in the village of Villiers-le-Bel.

The estate was owned by the Blumenthals, a middle-aged couple who had become close friends of the young Hassams. Madame Blumenthal, whose husband was a wealthy German businessman, was the daughter of the French painter Thomas Couture. A transitional figure between the discipline of the Academy and the freedom of Impressionism, Couture had taught Edouard Manet and numerous Americans, including Mary Cassatt. For Hassam, however, Couture's most significant pupil was Hunt, who had studied with the French master from 1846 to 1851. In happy anticipation of a visit to the Blumenthals, Hassam wrote to a friend, "I shall paint in a charming old French garden . . . where Couture lived and painted. Hunt must have been there."[1]

Hassam spent part of the summers of 1887–89 in Villiers-le-Bel, where his interest in country landscapes shifted from the farm to the garden.[2] Most of the

paintings he produced there depict a beautiful woman surrounded by carefully tended flowers. In *Peach Blossoms—Villiers-le-Bel,* by contrast, he depicted a neglected corner of an orchard. The Blumenthals' expert gardener, whose work Hassam so admired, must have given up caring for the tree depicted in this painting. Peach trees are traditionally pruned into a goblet shape to expose the ripening fruit to maximum sunlight. This specimen, however, was left to grow into a twiggy tangle. Hassam obviously enjoyed the visual dialogue between the bold simplicity of the Y-shaped trunk and the pleasing complexity of the interwoven twigs and delicate blossoms. His selection of this motif reveals both the persistence of his Barbizon-inspired preference for the homely and imperfect and a new fascination with Asian art.

A blossoming peach tree is a familiar subject in Chinese and Japanese art, where the contrast between old wood and young blossoms evokes poetic meditations on the passage of time. The Asian influence is also evident in Hassam's calligraphic brushwork, particularly in the branches and flowers on the upper right. His brushstrokes are greatly varied: energetic swoops delineate the branches, rounded dabs describe the petals, and vertical swipes of a square brush suggest the tall grass. In this early work, Hassam assimilated the aesthetic of Chinese and Japanese art far more thoroughly than in many of his later paintings, where his taste for Asian culture is indicated merely by the inclusion of fans, porcelains, folding screens, and other fashionable props.

Villiers-le-Bel offered Hassam an opportunity to engage with a theme that would become one of his most important. The paintings he created there, including *Peach Blossoms,* consolidated his shift to Impressionism and marked a new direction in his art.

1. Childe Hassam, Paris, June 27, 1888, to Miss Rose Lamb, Isles of Shoals; transcript in Ulrich W. Heisinger, *Childe Hassam: American Impressionist* (Munich and New York: Prestel, 1994), p. 178.
2. Hassam also visited Villiers-le-Bel during a trip to Europe in 1897.

11 ROBERT VONNOH (1858–1933)

The Bridge at Grez, ca. 1907–11
Oil on canvas, 36½ × 51⅜ inches
Gift of Mrs. Louis Lewison, 1970 (1970.149)

This evocative painting embodies two hallmarks of the art colony at Grez, on the river Loing south of Paris: the bridge that was the artists' favorite subject and the hazy atmosphere that enveloped the village and determined the palette of most of the paintings created there.

Grez-sur-Loing attracted a colony of American, British, and Scandinavian artists from about 1875 to 1890. About forty-four miles from Paris, Grez was located "within walking distance of Barbizon and a donkey ride from Fontainebleau," according to an 1879 guidebook.[1] The Scottish novelist Robert Louis Stevenson and his painter-cousin R. A. M. Stevenson were among the first English-speaking artists to discover the village. The Americans who painted there over the years include several in this exhibition: Robert Vonnoh, Theodore Robinson, Willard Metcalf, John Singer Sargent, Childe Hassam, and Ruger Donoho.

The old arched bridge over the Loing inspired so many paintings that Robert Louis Stevenson called it "a piece of public property; anonymously famous; beaming on the incurious dilettante from the walls of a hundred exhibitions."[2] Captured on canvas, the river valley's pearly light and stone architecture prompted numerous quips about the gray school of Grez, whose artists shared the preference for a monochromatic palette and subdued light that has been labeled Tonalist. The influence of Jean-Charles Cazin, the most distinguished French artist who worked in Grez, and of Jules Bastien-Lepage, who was internationally admired in the 1880s, reinforced that stylistic tendency.

When Vonnoh arrived in Grez in the autumn of 1887, he was already respected as an art teacher and portrait painter. Born in Hartford, Connecticut, he had grown up in Boston, where he attended the Massachusetts Normal Art School before going to Paris in 1881 for two years of study at the Académie Julian under Gustave-Rodolphe Boulanger and Jules-Joseph Lefebvre. On his return to Boston, Vonnoh joined the faculty of the School of the Museum of Fine Arts. He went back to France in 1887 accompanied by his wife, Grace Farrell Vonnoh, and took additional instruction at the Académie Julian before going to Grez-sur-Loing. He made that village his principal residence for the next four years and returned there periodically for the rest of his life.

The paintings Vonnoh produced in Grez between 1887 and 1891 include works in three distinct styles: dark-toned academic figure studies, muted Tonalist landscapes with figures, and—in a radical departure for Vonnoh—brightly hued landscapes painted in pure, unmixed colors. The latter, colorful views of poppy fields, were influenced by the most daring painter in the art colony, the Irishman Roderic O'Conor. Vonnoh later explained the dramatic new direction in his work: "I gradually came to realize the value of first impression and the necessity of correct value, pure color, and higher key, resulting in my soon becoming a devoted disciple of the new movement in painting."[3] His conversion was not complete, however; he continued to shift from a high-keyed to a more muted palette to appeal simultaneously to patrons who admired Impressionism and to those who deemed that style superficial. "Mr. Vonnoh has learned what he could from the impressionists, but he has learned more from nature itself," one critic wrote approvingly; "his work shows . . . that he looks deeper than the surface of things and can interpret to us something more than their outward aspect."[4]

Vonnoh returned to the United States in 1891. For the next five years, he taught at the Pennsylvania Academy of the Fine Arts, where his students included two in this exhibition—Edward Willis Redfield and Walter Elmer Schofield—as well as the urban realists Robert Henri, John Sloan, and William Glackens. For his students, Vonnoh was an important source of information about the latest developments in French painting.

After his first wife's death in 1899, Vonnoh married the sculptor Bessie Potter, whose portrait by William Merritt Chase is in this exhibition (no. 28). In 1907 the Vonnohs returned to France and rented a house by the river Loing that would be the painter's base for the next four years. The art colony had dispersed by then, and

FIGURE 8
Claude Monet, *Morning on the Seine, near Giverny,* 1897. Oil on canvas, 32 × 36½ inches. Museum of Fine Arts, Boston; Gift of Mrs. W. Scott Fitz

Bessie Potter Vonnoh, who was not fluent in French, spent most of her time in the United States, but her husband could hardly bear to leave the quiet village. *Bridge at Grez,* the most significant painting of Vonnoh's second extended stay there, seems to represent a return to the gray school. However, its soft palette, diffused light, and interest in reflections link it to Claude Monet's *Morning on the Seine, near Giverny* (fig. 8), part of a series the French Impressionist had painted in 1896–97. As Monet had done, Vonnoh suppressed any evidence of modern life. He allowed no boats, vehicles, or costumed figures to disturb the tranquility or to disclose the date. Responding to the familiar view from the end of his garden, Vonnoh instead monumentalized the bridge as a timeless emblem of the French heritage, tying the man-made structure to its natural setting in a pattern of ovals formed by three of the arches and their reflections in the placid water.

1. May Alcott Nieriker, *Studying Art Abroad and How to Do It Cheaply* (Boston, 1879), p. 60; quoted in May Brawley Hill, "Robert Vonnoh: Academic Impressionist," unpublished paper (files, Department of American Paintings and Sculpture, The Metropolitan Museum of Art, New York, 1982), p. 7. I am also indebted to May Brawley Hill, *Grez Days: Robert Vonnoh in France,* exhibition catalogue (New York: Berry-Hill Galleries, 1987), which is the authoritative study of Vonnoh.

2. Robert Louis Stevenson, "Fontainebleau: Village Communities of Painters," *Magazine of Art* 7 (1884), p. 341.

3. Quoted in *National Cyclopedia of American Biography* 7 (New York: J.T. White, 1897), p. 462.

4. Lucy Monroe, "Chicago Letter," *Critic* 24 (March 17, 1894), p. 190.

WALTER ELMER SCHOFIELD (1867–1944)

Sand Dunes near Lelant, Cornwall, England, 1905

Oil on canvas, 38 × 48 inches
George A. Hearn Fund, 1909 (09.26.1)

Schofield occupies an unusual position in any discussion of American painters abroad. The son of English immigrants to the United States (his mother was the grandniece of Mary Wollstonecraft Shelley, the author of *Frankenstein*), he married an English woman and settled permanently in her homeland in 1897. Unlike most other expatriates, however, he held his American and British ties in remarkably even balance. He spent roughly half of every year in the United States; he was identified with art colonies in both Pennsylvania and Cornwall, England; he was a member of both the National Academy of Design and the Royal Society of British Artists; and he divided his attention between winter landscapes painted in Pennsylvania and views of the Cornish coast.[1]

A native of Philadelphia, Schofield studied at the Pennsylvania Academy of the Fine Arts from 1889 to 1892 under Robert Vonnoh. While a student at the academy, he became friends with Robert Henri, John Sloan, William Glackens, and the sculptor Charles Grafly. Late in 1892 Schofield sailed for Paris, where he studied at the Académie Julian under William Bouguereau, Gabriel Ferrier, and Henri-Lucien Doucet, and later at the Académie Colarossi under François Aman-Jean. He practiced landscape painting during sketching trips in France and Holland with Henri, Glackens, and Grafly. On his return to Philadelphia in 1895, Schofield joined the circle of artists who gathered on Tuesday evenings at Henri's studio. That group included the landscapist Edward Willis Redfield and the painters whose unidealized views of working-class New York would earn them the label the Ashcan school: Henri, Sloan, Glackens, George Luks, and Everett Shinn.

In 1897 Schofield married Muriel Redmayne, a British citizen who had been visiting Philadelphia with her parents. Because his wife disliked the United States, they settled in England, but Schofield returned home alone every year. His painting forays in Pennsylvania led to the emergence of his mature style in 1904. That year, as in the two previous winters, he stayed with his close friend Redfield, who had already developed a vigorous, painterly technique that married Henri's Realism to Impressionist themes. Redfield described to Schofield a winter landscape he planned to paint from his front yard for the Carnegie Institute's prestigious annual exhibition. Back in his studio in England, Schofield painted the same scene from memory in a newly bold manner that owed much to his Pennsylvania host. He submitted the canvas to the Carnegie exhibition, where it won the Medal of the First Class. Redfield was outraged, and the two artists became bitter enemies.

Sand Dunes near Lelant typifies the realistic style, large canvases, expansive vistas, and rural subject matter for which Schofield became famous. He created it while he was living in a small rented house at St. Ives, Cornwall, a picturesque fishing community that had attracted a colony of landscape painters. The area was rugged, quiet, and unspoiled. A contemporary guidebook advised, "If the visitor has a desire to . . . spend most of the day out of doors on the sea, sands, or cliffs, and to feel thankful at night for the oblivion of restful sleep; or if he wants to read, or to sketch, or to paint," St. Ives was ideal.[2]

This picture depicts the nearby village of Lelant, on the estuary of the Hayle River not far from the artist's studio. (Today, the site is occupied by an electricity generating plant.[3]) Lelant was veiled in an aura of romance and mystery because of the fierce sandstorms that, according to one old chronicle, had "choaked the harbour and buried much of the lande and houses." Tradition held that an extensive town lay buried beneath the sand near the church.[4] Schofield focused attention in the foreground on the notorious sand, which resembles the snow he painted in Pennsylvania. His panoramic view embraces other characteristics of the Cornish landscape: the whitewashed village, the distant river, and the blue-green moors rising to a moody sky.

Schofield was unable to leave England during World War II. Homesick for his native land, he died in Cornwall and was buried in Lelant. Even in death, his dual allegiances were evident: after the war, his remains were disinterred and reburied in Philadelphia.

1. The biographical information is based on Thomas C. Folk, *Walter Elmer Schofield: Bold Impressionist,* exhibition catalogue (Chadds Ford, Pa.: Brandywine River Museum, 1983), and Folk, *The Pennsylvania Impressionists* (London: Associated University Presses, 1997), pp. 52–61.

2. *Penzance, St. Ives, Land's End and the Scilly Isles,* 6th ed. (London: Ward, Lock and Co., ca. 1906), p. 74.

3. Sydney E. Schofield to Doreen Bolger Burke, Cornwall, May 26, 1980, artist's file, Department of American Paintings and Sculpture, The Metropolitan Museum of Art.

4. *Penzance, St. Ives, Land's End and the Scilly Isles,* p. 74.

Alpine Pool, ca. 1907

Oil on canvas, 27½ × 38 inches
Gift of Mrs. Francis Ormond, 1950 (50.130.15)

Throughout his life, Sargent traveled widely, finding subjects for his art in locales as diverse as Spain, Norway, and Egypt. In his youth, he and his family had escaped the heat and threat of malaria in Florence by summering in the Alps. As an adult, Sargent returned to the mountains nearly every year between 1902 and 1914, accompanied by a lively coterie of relatives and friends. Those holidays resulted in some of his most personal and appealing pictures.

Sargent's Alpine retreat from 1904 to 1908 was the remote hamlet of Purtud in northwestern Italy near the borders of France and Switzerland. Set in the enclosed Val de Veny, Purtud was watered by a small, snow-fed brook, which, in the summer of 1907, claimed the attention of Sargent and his party. The icy stream challenged the hardiness of the artist's young nephews, who bathed boisterously there every morning. "The children look so jolly rushing around the sunny meadow, naked and rolling in the cristal water," the artist Jane de Glehn, who was a member of Sargent's cohort that summer, wrote to her mother.[1]

In the same letter, de Glehn related that Sargent was using the brook as a motif in his paintings. "Yesterday I spent all day posing . . . in Turkish costume for Sargent on the mossy banks of the brook," she wrote. "He is doing a harem disporting itself on the banks of the stream. He has stacks of lovely Oriental clothes and dresses anyone he can get in them."[2] Sargent had long been fascinated by the mystery, sensuality, and exoticism of the Middle East, which he had visited most recently in 1905. In preparation for his painting holiday in the Alps two years later, he packed trunks full of opulent costumes, which he used to create fantasy images of odalisques and Turks in the unlikely setting of an Alpine meadow. Orientalist subject matter had been popular in Europe throughout the eighteenth and nineteenth centuries. Sargent's innovation was to take the theme outdoors, removing it from the shadowy interiors of palaces and bathhouses to the banks of a sparkling mountain stream, as in the painting *Dolce Far Niente* (fig. 9).

FIGURE 9
John Singer Sargent, *Dolce Far Niente,* ca. 1909–10. Oil on canvas, 16⁵⁄₁₆ × 28⁵⁄₁₆ inches. Brooklyn Museum of Art; Bequest of A. Augustus Healy

Sargent also used the brook as a subject in its own right, studying its constantly shifting patterns of light and shadow in a series of oils and watercolors that includes the brilliant *Alpine Pool.* Although it is a pure landscape, *Alpine Pool* shares many characteristics with *Dolce Far Niente.* For both the landscape and the figurative painting, Sargent employed vibrant colors to capture the kaleidoscopic surface patterns produced by strong contrasts of light and shadow. He adopted the same close-up vantage point, gazing down at the bank of the stream just beyond his easel. And in both canvases, he eliminated the horizon line and minimized spatial recession to intensify focus on the central motif. In *Alpine Pool,* without the complications of exotically garbed figures, the viewer—like the artist—can be utterly absorbed in the play of light over rocks, foliage, and water.

---

1. Jane de Glehn to her mother, Mrs. W. J. Emmet, August 13, 1907; quoted by Richard Ormond in Warren Adelson et al., *Sargent Abroad: Figures and Landscapes* (New York: Abbeville Press, 1997), p. 68.
2. Ibid., p. 84.

Afternoon Among the Cypress, ca. 1905

Oil on canvas, 26¼ × 30 inches
Gift of Mrs. Henrietta Zeile, 1909 (09.186)

Arthur Frank Mathews is the only artist in this exhibition who based his entire career in the American West. (Colin Campbell Cooper retired to California after spending most of his adult life in New York.) When asked why he remained in San Francisco instead of moving to one of the eastern art centers, Mathews replied, "California is an undiscovered country for the painter. It hasn't been touched. The forms and colors of our countryside haven't begun to yield their secrets."[1]

Born in Wisconsin, Mathews moved with his family to Oakland, California, when he was six years old. He apprenticed in his father's architectural office and studied privately with the local artist Henry Bruen. From 1881 to 1884 he worked in San Francisco as a graphic designer and illustrator, saving his money for further study in France. He left for Paris in 1885; for the next four years, he studied at the Académie Julian under Gustave-Rodolphe Boulanger and Jules-Joseph Lefebvre. Their emphasis on figure drawing perfectly suited the young artist. In 1886 he won the Academy's medal for distinction in composition, drawing, and painting. The following year, his painting *Imogen and Arviragus* (1887; Oakland Museum of California), illustrating a scene in Shakespeare's play *Cymbeline,* was accepted at the Salon. For the rest of Mathews's career, figurative subjects inspired by literature, history, mythology, or allegory would be the mainstays of his art.

On his return to San Francisco in the late summer of 1889, Mathews assumed a leading role in the city's cultural life. He taught life class at the San Francisco Art Students League and joined the faculty of the California School of Design, which he would serve as director from 1890 until 1906. (The school was renamed the Mark Hopkins Institute of Art in 1893.) Mathews patterned the art school on the Parisian model, emphasizing figure drawing and the study of anatomy. He married one of his students, Lucia Kleinhans, in 1894. She would often be his collaborator on the murals he painted for San Francisco homes, banks, clubs, and offices. With large areas of flat color, those decorative works reveal the influence of the contemporary French painter Pierre Puvis de Chavannes as well as of the Japanese prints that Mathews collected.

For respite from city life, Mathews frequently traveled south to the Monterey peninsula, where he painted the spectacular landscape. If Mathews's figurative paintings were rooted in the European past, his landscapes celebrate California's distinctive topography, plant life, and light. For this canvas, he chose as his subject one of California's most familiar natural emblems: a species of cypress indigenous to the bluffs surrounding Monterey Bay. On the Seventeen Mile Drive in Monterey, the tree is commemorated in five of the twenty-two landmarks, including the famous Lone Cypress, a gnarled and windswept survivor on a rocky outcropping over the crashing surf. Probably referring to this painting, a critic for the *San Francisco Chronicle* wrote in 1905: "Before a picture which Mathews calls 'The Cypress,' one may easily stand in something akin to a reverent attitude, for in this, one of the very best things Mathews has painted, the wonder of the trees is told and the atmosphere is fine and free and appealing. This picture gives one the desire to pack his grip and get out into the temples made of trees."[2]

The artist's sense of place inspired not only the subject but also the palette of this painting. As in his murals, Mathews used flat, unmodulated areas of color, but the tawny golden tonality is typically Californian. Keenly sensitive to the characteristic light of the locale, Matthews explained: "I never work outside until after 4 o'clock in the afternoon . . . for to me the most extraordinary color effects that we find here in the West come only in the diffused afternoon lights."[3]

After the devastating San Francisco earthquake and fire of 1906, Mathews was a leader in the reconstruction movement. He resigned from the Mark Hopkins Institute, headed the committee for the distribution of relief funds to the city's artists, and designed and built the first studios constructed after the fire. Those studios housed the magazine *Philopolis,* which featured articles (many of them written and illustrated by Mathews) on art and city planning; the Philopolis Press, with books designed and illustrated by Arthur and Lucia Mathews; and the Furniture Shop, which until 1920 employed as many as fifty craftworkers in the production of furniture, frames, and decorative objects. *Afternoon Among the Cypress* was donated to the Metropolitan Museum by the mother of John Zeile, Mathews's business partner in the Furniture Shop.

1. Quoted in Harvey L. Jones, *Mathews: Masterpieces of the California Decorative Style,* exhibition catalogue (Oakland, Calif.: The Oakland Museum, 1972), p. 42.

2. *San Francisco Chronicle,* March 13, 1905, p. 7.

3. Quoted in Jones, *Mathews,* p. 42.

August, ca. 1908

Oil on canvas, 29 x 36½ inches
Gift of George A. Hearn, 1909 (09.72.3)

"If you do not love skies sufficiently to observe and study them as you would the figure or the other elements of landscape, put up your horizon line or otherwise eliminate the sky as an important feature of your work, for you cannot fill large spaces with interest without earnest, patient, loving study."[1] So Charles H. Davis advised beginning artists in an essay published the year after he completed this painting. By then, the "earnest, patient, loving study" of clouds had been his specialty for about fifteen years. Davis's attention to clouds accompanied his shift from the Barbizon-inspired Tonalism of his earlier work to the Impressionism of *August*.

Davis first saw Barbizon paintings at the Boston Athenaeum in 1874. He was initially disappointed by the works of Jean-François Millet and his colleagues. In fact, he confessed later, he was "indignant that such commonplace things should be thrust upon me as attractions in what I expected was to be a high class affair and for which I had paid my entrance fee of fifty cents."[2] However, Davis soon came to admire Barbizon art so much that it strengthened his determination to become a painter.

Davis began his training at a free drawing school in Boston, then studied for three years at the newly opened School of the Museum of Fine Arts before returning to his hometown of Amesbury, Massachusetts, to earn his living as a portrait draftsman. When a local businessman learned of the young artist's ambition to study in Paris, he gave him one thousand dollars, enabling him to sail for France in 1880. Davis enrolled at the Académie Julian under Jules-Joseph Lefebvre and Gustave-Rodolphe Boulanger, but dropped out after visiting Barbizon, the village on the edge of the Forest of Fontainebleau where Millet, Théodore Rousseau, Camille Corot, and others painted.

Davis married a French woman, Angèle-Geneviève Legarde, and remained in France for ten years. The canvases he exhibited in the Paris Salons beginning in 1881 typically featured bleak autumnal landscapes rendered in a somber palette without vivid contrasts of light and shadow. He later told an interviewer that, during his sojourn in France, he had seen a picture by Claude Monet in a shop window in Paris and had instantly "understood what Monet was trying to relate."[3] However, it was not until after he returned to the United States that Davis adopted Impressionism. That shift seems to have been inspired more by the landscape and artists of Connecticut than by the French painter.

Davis returned to America in 1890, and settled two years later in Mystic, a small town on Connecticut's coast about halfway between Boston and New York. The bright light and hilly, rock-strewn countryside were dramatically different from the murky woods, flat farmland, and peasant villages of the Barbizon region. Davis's intimate, even claustrophobic French forest interiors were replaced by expansive vistas of rolling fields crowned by windswept clouds. The example of other artists then working in Connecticut validated this stylistic and thematic shift. Since about 1890, an art colony in Cos Cob had attracted artists including John H. Twachtman, J. Alden Weir, Childe Hassam, and Theodore Robinson. Davis would have seen their work in New York exhibitions, if not in Connecticut. He in turn passed on this influence to the summer students who came to Mystic to work under his instruction. (Three years after his first wife died in 1894, Davis married one of those students, Frances Darby Thomas.)

Davis advised young artists to observe the effect of the wind on cloud shapes to capture the "rhythmic movement" that was the essential character of the subject. In *August*, the play of light over earth and sky conveys an effect of motion. The distant hills are bathed in brilliant sunshine, while a thundercloud darkens the middle ground and advances toward the viewer. Unlike many artists, whose cottony daubs of clouds seem like afterthoughts in their landscapes, Davis achieved a credible illusion of depth as a result of his treatment of the sky. The most distant clouds—those low on the horizon—are the smallest, while those nearest the viewer loom high in the foreground.

Davis did not completely repudiate his Barbizon manner when he adopted Impressionism but seems to have alternated styles in response to his patrons' preferences. When the distinguished collector William T. Evans asked him to send a painting to an exhibition of works by artist-members of New York's Lotos Club, Davis was torn between two canvases. Knowing Evans's affinity for such American Tonalists as George Inness, he considered sending an oil titled *Sunset Clouds* rather than *August*. "The former may be a little more Lotos Club & stand less chance of being hung in some outside overflow place it being quite properly *tonal* in character," he told his dealer, William Macbeth. In the end, however, he chose *August* to represent him, explaining to Macbeth that "it seemed to be considered one of my best things." Davis also realized that one of "these summer cloud subjects . . . would naturally be expected of me."[4] Shortly after the exhibition opened, the collector George A. Hearn purchased *August* for the Metropolitan Museum, of which he was a trustee.

1. Charles H. Davis, "A Study of Clouds," *Palette and Bench* 1 (September 1909), p. 262.

2. This quotation and much of the biographical information on Davis are taken from Thomas L. Colville, *Charles Harold Davis, N.A. 1856–1933,* exhibition catalogue (Mystic, Conn.: Mystic Art Association, 1982).

3. Rochelle Brackman, "Noted Landscape Artist Lived 43 Years in State," *Hartford Courant*, October 8, 1933, unpaged clipping, artist's file, Department of American Paintings and Sculpture, The Metropolitan Museum of Art.

4. Davis to Macbeth, February 2 and 23, 1909, Archives of American Art, Smithsonian Institution, Washington, D.C., roll NMc6, frames 668–69 and 572–75; quoted in Doreen Bolger, "William Macbeth and George A. Hearn: Collecting American Art, 1903–1910," *Archives of American Art Journal* 15, no. 2 (1975), p. 13.

Hillside Pastures, 1922

Oil on canvas, 26 × 28⅞ inches

Bequest of Miss Adelaide Milton de Groot (1876–1967), 1967 (67.187.134)

"I shall once more pack up my things to go to Vermont—up to Chester," Willard Metcalf wrote to his ten-year-old daughter Rosalind on August 6, 1922, adding, "I want to paint the springtime up there— with the beautiful hills and dancing, singing brooks."[1] But Metcalf did not wait until spring to paint the bucolic countryside around Chester, which is situated between two branches of the Williams River in southern Vermont. *Hillside Pastures* is one of a group of landscapes he completed there in the autumn of 1922.

It was not the first time Metcalf had painted in Chester. He had probably initially seen the picturesque village on his way north to Cornish, New Hampshire, where he was a frequent visitor between 1909 and 1920. He spent two months in Chester in 1920, based at the Fullerton Inn on the town green. He returned to the inn on September 26, 1922. His old friend Frank W. Benson joined him for a week or two of trout fishing and painting, after which Metcalf stayed on alone to paint the rolling landscape.

The pictures that Metcalf produced in the vicinity of Chester during the last three years of his life have been recognized as among his finest. When a group of them, including *Hillside Pastures,* was shown in a solo retrospective at the Corcoran Gallery of Art in 1925, the author of the catalogue essay described Metcalf as "the poet laureate of these homely hills."[2] In a review of that exhibition, the critic for the *Washington Post* acclaimed Metcalf as "one of those who has placed an indelible stamp upon American art, and who will leave behind him . . . for the uplift and joy of future generations a priceless heritage."[3] Exhilarated by such glowing reviews, Metcalf wrote to his dealer Albert Milch that he intended "to go out and paint better than ever."[4] However, he died of a heart attack on March 8, 1925.

By the time of Metcalf's death, Impressionism had long since lost its position on the cutting edge of American art. The New York Realists, led by Robert Henri, combined the expressive brushwork and dark palette of the seventeenth-century Dutch and Spanish masters Frans Hals, Rembrandt, and Diego Velázquez with gritty urban imagery, but even their innovations seemed timid in the wake of the Armory Show of 1913. The European modernist paintings in that immense exhibition confounded Americans' preconceptions of how art should look. Metcalf's wife recalled later that when they visited the "Cubists show," as Metcalf referred to it in his diary, he nearly fainted from the shock.[5] While many American artists were profoundly influenced by the works they saw at the Armory Show, Metcalf continued to produce genteel, highly realistic canvases in an Impressionist style.

Born in Lowell, Massachusetts, where his parents worked in the mills, Metcalf grew up mostly in the Boston area. At sixteen, he was apprenticed to a wood engraver and began evening classes in drawing at the Massachusetts Normal Art School. An apprenticeship to the landscape painter George Loring Brown and life classes at the Lowell Institute followed. In 1876 he entered the newly established School of the Museum of Fine Arts, Boston, on a full scholarship. After completing his studies at the Museum School in 1879, Metcalf supported himself as an illustrator, saving his money for study in Europe. He achieved that goal when he sailed for France in 1883. Like many of his compatriots, he studied under Gustave-Rodolphe Boulanger and Jules-Joseph Lefebvre at the Académie Julian. Among his fellow students were John H. Twachtman, Frank Benson, and Childe Hassam, who would become lifelong friends. Metcalf spent holidays painting in the artists' colonies at Pont-Aven in Brittany and Grez-Sur-Loing near the Forest of Fontainebleau. He was one of the first Americans to visit Giverny, where he spent extended periods between 1886 and 1888, sharing a house with Theodore Robinson and collecting botanical specimens with Monet's son.

Metcalf returned to the United States in late December 1888, settling the following year in New York. For the next few years he supported himself through teaching, portrait commissions, and work as an illustrator. In 1904, penniless and ill, he retreated from his hard-drinking New York social milieu to his parents' home in Maine. During nearly a year of painting in relative isolation, he embraced the subject matter with which he would be identified: the New England landscape. Metcalf returned to New York from his personal "Renaissance," as he called it, but for the rest of his life, he escaped the city at every opportunity to work in the countryside.

In America as in Europe, Metcalf gravitated to artists' colonies. He painted in Old Lyme, Connecticut, between 1903 and 1907, and in Cornish, New Hampshire, between 1909 and 1920. The colony in Cornish was self-consciously aesthetic, staging elaborate theatrical entertainments and formal dinner parties. Metcalf soon discovered that he preferred Cornish in the winter, when the other artists had returned to New York. In the last five years of his life, avoiding art colonies entirely, he made Chester his primary base for painting. While winter was his preferred season in Cornish, spring and fall often found him in Chester.

Some critics considered Metcalf's work excessively realistic in the years after the Armory Show, but others appreciated his sense of place and ability to evoke the American past. "Take almost any of his landscapes," observed the writer of his obituary in the *New York Tribune,* "and in a trice the picture seems to carry you into the heart of some individualized spot in pastoral America. It wakes old memories. The very spirit of our soil is in it."[6]

1. Willard Metcalf to Rosalind Metcalf, place not specified, August 6, 1922; quoted in Elizabeth de Veer and Richard J. Boyle, *Sunlight and Shadow: The Life and Art of Willard L. Metcalf* (New York: Abbeville Press, 1987), p. 141.

2. Walter Jack Duncan, *Paintings by Willard L. Metcalf,* exhibition catalogue (Washington, D.C.: The Corcoran Gallery of Art, 1925), unpaged.

3. *Washington Post,* January 11, 1925; quoted in de Veer and Boyle, *Sunlight and Shadow,* p. 243.

4. De Veer and Boyle, *Sunlight and Shadow,* p. 155.

5. Ibid., p. 106.

6. "Willard Metcalf," *New York Tribune,* March 10, 1925, clipping in artist's file, Department of American Paintings and Sculpture, The Metropolitan Museum of Art.

17 EDWARD WILLIS REDFIELD (1869–1965)

Overlooking the Valley, 1911
Oil on canvas, 31⅞ × 39⁵⁄₁₆ inches
Gift of Mrs. E. H. Harriman, 1916 (16.150)

Edward Willis Redfield was the most prominent of the Pennsylvania Impressionists. He attracted many painters to the area around New Hope in Bucks County and was a major influence on the winter landscapes for which those artists are best known.[1]

Redfield came to know and love the rural landscape of the Delaware River valley during boyhood vacations from his family home in Philadelphia. His artistic training, however, was directed toward a career as a portrait painter. From 1887 to 1889 he studied at the Pennsylvania Academy of the Fine Arts. His teachers, Thomas Anshutz, James Kelly, and Thomas Hovenden, emphasized figure painting grounded in thorough knowledge of anatomy. The academy's tradition of direct treatment of unidealized subjects, based on the precepts of Thomas Eakins, affected Redfield's art even after he abandoned figure painting. His commitment to realism was reinforced by his friendship with fellow student Robert Henri, who would remain an important influence on his artistic development.

Redfield sailed for France in August 1889, about one year after Henri. Following his friend's lead, Redfield joined the popular class at the Académie Julian taught by William Bouguereau and Tony Robert-Fleury. Rather than emulating his teachers' preference for academic nudes in mythological guises, the young American was attracted to the work of the Impressionists. Instead of copying the old masters at the Louvre, he haunted the Luxembourg Museum, where he studied landscapes by Claude Monet, Camille Pissarro, and the Norwegian painter Fritz Thaulow. Redfield tried his hand at landscape during sketching trips with Henri to Pont-Aven in 1889 and the Mediterranean coast in 1890. In 1891 they visited the Forest of Fontainebleau, staying at the

Hôtel Deligant in the village of Bois-le-Roi. There Redfield painted his first snow scene, *Canal en hiver,* which was accepted for the Salon of 1891. There, too, he met the innkeeper's daughter, Elise Devin Deligant, whom he married two years later.

The newlyweds settled in the Philadelphia suburb of Glenside, and Redfield joined a group of artists who met on Tuesday evenings at Henri's Philadelphia studio. Henri's circle included the sculptors Charles Grafly and Alexander Stirling Calder, who were friends from the Pennsylvania Academy; the landscape painter Walter Elmer Schofield; and the newspaper illustrators John Sloan, William Glackens, Everett Shinn, and George Luks. The charismatic Henri's influence was most pronounced on the latter group, who, inspired by his example, took up painting, moved to New York, and devoted themselves to capturing the raw energy of the city. Henri's demand for vigorous brushwork and straightforward realism also had a profound impact on the Pennsylvania landscapists Redfield and Schofield.

In 1898 the Redfields bought a house on the towpath of the Delaware Canal in Center Bridge, Pennsylvania, just across the Delaware River from Stockton, New Jersey. Unlike most artists at the time, Redfield painted outdoors during the winter and reserved summers for gardening, carpentry, and other do-it-yourself projects. He became nearly self-sufficient, keeping a cow, a pig, and chickens and growing vegetables for the family's table. That spirit of rugged individuality extended to his art. He worked outdoors in severe weather conditions, lashing his canvases to the trees so he could paint during storms. He completed each canvas in a single day, never reworking it in the studio. "Either you've got it the first time or you haven't," he declared.[2] What

he aimed to "get" was the appearance of a barn or a hillside on a specific day.

Redfield found most of his subjects within walking distance of his home. *Overlooking the Valley* depicts a view down to the Delaware River and across it to New Jersey. In a skillful use of the complementary colors yellow and violet, the artist contrasts the golden grass exposed by the melting snow in the foreground with the violet hills in the distance. The canvas exemplifies the realism for which Redfield was praised; the ordinary frame houses and outbuildings viewed through a screen of tangled underbrush are rendered honestly with no attempt to prettify them. Viewed up close, however, the painting dissolves into an abstract web of contrasting textures: the snow at the right, smoothly laid on with a palette knife, is juxtaposed with the nervous, wiry lines of grass, twigs, and branches.

In the years surrounding World War I, paintings such as *Overlooking the Valley* were deemed to embody American values of "manly" vigor and unadorned realism. The earlier work of artists such as Twachtman and Robinson seemed too genteel and too European to Americans whose cultural self-confidence—and isolationism—was growing. When, in 1909, the French government bought Redfield's *February,* the critic Frank Jewett Mather hailed the purchase as the triumph of an American spirit in art.[3] Until then, most American paintings acquired for the Luxembourg Museum— by the expatriates John Singer Sargent and James McNeill Whistler, for example—were cosmopolitan in theme and technique. In contrast, Redfield's subject (a Pennsylvania towpath) and method ("a crisp, direct naturalism"), were, Mather observed, "emphatically our kind of thing."

---

1. The best source on Redfield is Thomas C. Folk, *The Pennsylvania Impressionists* (London: Associated University Presses, 1997).
2. Quoted in Barbara Pollack, "Bucks County Since He Moved There 65 years Ago," *Philadelphia Sunday Bulletin Magazine,* August 4, 1963, p. 9.
3. Frank Jewett Mather, Jr., "The Luxembourg and American Painting," *Scribner's Magazine* 47 (March 1910), p. 381.

American Impressionists in Their Professional Environments

Connecticut Village, after 1891

Oil on canvas, 24⅛ × 20⅛ inches

Bequest of Miss Adelaide Milton de Groot (1876–1967), 1967 (67.187.143)

Connecticut Village, painted in a sketchy style very different from that of *Fruit* (no. 26), reveals Weir's shift to Impressionism, a stylistic choice that was closely linked to his sojourns in the Connecticut countryside. (For his biography, see number 26.) Weir acquired a 150-acre farm in the western Connecticut hamlet of Branchville in 1882. The following year, when he married Anna Dwight Baker, he gained an additional country retreat: the Bakers' farm in Windham, about thirty miles east of Hartford. For the rest of his life, Weir spent much of each year in Connecticut. There he found the subjects for his landscapes and enjoyed the stimulus of colleagues who came to visit or who lived nearby.

Weir seems not to have adopted a modified Impressionism until about 1887, when his close friend John H. Twachtman rented a house near the Branchville farm. Together, the two artists experimented in pastel and etching. When Twachtman settled in nearby Greenwich in 1889, these collaborative investigations intensified. Twachtman and Weir were often joined by other colleagues, including Childe Hassam and Theodore Robinson, who came to paint with them in Branchville, Greenwich, and Cos Cob. Painting in the same vicinity during the day and discussing their work in the evening, they shared insights newborn at the easel. Each took a different direction, but each supported and stimulated the others' innovations.

Weir Farm in Branchville is now a National Historic Site. Windham's role in Weir's art has received less attention, but he produced some of his finest paintings there. In *The Red Bridge* (ca. 1895; The Metropolitan Museum of Art, New York) and the factory village series, he depicted industrial incursions in the state's rural northeast corner.[1] In *Connecticut Village*, on the other hand, he portrayed a modest street in Windham Center. The town celebrated its bicentennial in 1892, about the time Weir painted this portrait of the place.[2]

The site was as familiar to him as his own front yard. He set his easel close to the Baker mansion, whose carriage house appears at the right edge of the canvas. The Bakers' tenant house, known today as Weir Cottage, stood out of sight to the artist's left. The tree-lined lane that unwinds on a gentle diagonal leads into the southern end of the town green. Now called Weir Court, the street is lined with eighteenth- and early-nineteenth-century houses. The small white building in the distance was the post office. Weir made it the focal point of his composition, as it was for local residents who gathered there twice a day to collect their mail.

Weir's vantage point enabled him to ignore the Second Congregational Church, barely out of view on the right. Built in 1887, the new church would have compromised the sense of enduring tradition Weir honors in this painting. With its landmark steeple, the church would also have distorted the intimate scale of this unassuming scene. Vertical accents are provided instead by the elms and maples whose interlacing branches fill the top half of the canvas. The central placement of one tree recalls similar compositional strategies in the Japanese woodcuts and illustrated books Weir collected. Moreover, the sheltering trees suggest the harmony between humans and nature that made the country village so appealing to the artist.

The site was so significant to Weir that he depicted it at least two more times: in *Suburban Village* (ca. 1902–5; Phoenix Art Museum) and *Windham Village* (ca. 1913–14; St. Louis Art Museum). *Connecticut Village* is imbued with the sense of place that was an important component of American Impressionism.

1. Weir's *Red Bridge* and his factory images are discussed in their historical context in H. Barbara Weinberg, Doreen Bolger, and David Park Curry, *American Impressionism and Realism: The Painting of Modern Life, 1885–1915,* exhibition catalogue (New York: The Metropolitan Museum of Art, 1994), pp. 25–26 and 83–85.

2. For identifying the site of the painting and providing valuable information on Weir's life in Windham, I am indebted to municipal historian Ruth Ridgeway and independent scholar Hildegard Cummings. Letters from Ruth Ridgeway to Susan G. Larkin, December 1 and 12, 1997, and February 19, 1998; letters from Hildegard Cummings to Susan G. Larkin, December 8, 1997, and March 16, 1998.

19 JOHN H. TWACHTMAN (1853–1902)

Horseneck Falls, ca. 1889–1900

Oil on canvas, 30 × 25 inches
Bequest of Miss Adelaide Milton de Groot (1876–1967), 1967 (67.187.142)

"This is it!" John H. Twachtman exclaimed on his first sight of Horseneck Falls in Greenwich, Connecticut.[1] So enchanted was he with the meandering Horseneck Brook and its small cascade that he purchased a modest farmhouse nearby in February 1890. For a decade, he made his home ground his principal motif. Tirelessly exploring this quiet landscape, Twachtman created a body of intensely personal paintings that were recognized by his contemporaries as highly original.

Twachtman arrived at the signature style of his so-called Greenwich period after two earlier phases marked by the contrasting approaches of his European training. The son of German immigrants, he began his artistic education in his native Cincinnati. In 1875 he accompanied his teacher Frank Duveneck to Munich, where he studied at the Royal Academy of Fine Arts but was more affected by the vigorous brushwork and somber palette associated with the circle of the Realist painter Wilhelm Leibl. In Munich, he became friends with fellow student William Merritt Chase. Accompanied by Chase and Duveneck, Twachtman spent much of 1877 in Venice. Years later, showing a dark painting of the canals to a friend, Twachtman commented wryly, "That is sunny Venice, done under the influence of the Munich school."[2]

Twachtman returned to Cincinnati in 1879. Despite his chronically straitened finances, he would visit Europe frequently over the next few years. In 1880 he taught with Duveneck in Florence, continuing with "Duveneck's Boys" to Venice, where they met the expatriate American artist James McNeill Whistler. In Venice, Whistler was engaged in creating a suite of etchings and pastels, whose delicacy of touch and economy of means profoundly influenced Twachtman. After their marriage in 1881, Twachtman and his bride traveled in Holland and Belgium, accompanied at times by their good friends J. Alden Weir and his older half-brother John Ferguson Weir. During this trip, Twachtman became familiar with works by painters of the contemporary Hague School and the French painter

Jules Bastien-Lepage. Their example provided further impetus for Twachtman to lighten his palette and modify the heavy impasto favored in Munich.

In his determination to shed the Munich style and improve his drawing skills, Twachtman sailed for France in 1883 with his wife and their first child. At the Académie Julian in Paris, he met other American artists who would become lifelong friends, including three who are represented in this exhibition: Willard Metcalf, Frank W. Benson, and Edmund C. Tarbell. Twachtman honed his draftsmanship in Paris and refined his painting during summers in the countryside. In their silvery hues, thinly applied paint, and suggestions of the influence of Japanese art, the works of his French period reveal his debt to Whistler.

After two years in Paris, Twachtman returned to the Midwest. However, he was eager to move to the East Coast to enjoy the stimulation of other artists and greater opportunities to exhibit and sell his work. More important, he sought a landscape that would suit his preference for nature on a small scale. By 1889 he had settled on the unassuming Greenwich property that would inspire most of his finest paintings. The brighter colors and freer brushwork of the Greenwich canvases, by comparison with those he had created earlier, demonstrate Twachtman's selective adaptation of Impressionism.

In his attraction to intimate, familiar subject matter, Twachtman shared the cultivated taste of his period. A generation earlier, Americans had favored artistic visions of awe-inspiring grandeur. Crowds had flocked to see Frederic Edwin Church's seven-foot-wide painting of Niagara Falls (1857; The Corcoran Gallery of Art, Washington, D.C.) when it was exhibited in New York, Boston, and the South in the late 1850s; thousands more knew the work through a three-foot-wide chromolithograph. But Americans' relation with the landscape changed in the decades between Church's *Niagara* and Twachtman's *Horseneck Falls*. In the 1898 publication *Nature for Its Own Sake*, author

John C. Van Dyke celebrated the endless fascination of small cascades while dismissing Niagara as "merely a great horror of nature."[3] The "little waterfall, so delicate in its play, we may watch for hours, and afterward hear its low murmur in our ears whenever we choose to think about it," he wrote, "but its charm soon vanishes when it becomes a cataract."[4] With the closing of the frontier, the development of a heterogeneous population as a result of unprecedented immigration, the radical shift of people from agrarian settings to the cities, and the subsequent development of the suburbs, Americans increasingly turned inward, away from these daunting new realities. Instead of the awesome cataract that was a public spectacle in both its natural and its painted form, they preferred places that they could enjoy in solitude.

For Twachtman, Horseneck Falls was just such a place. Although the demands of supporting a large family forced him to spend two or three days a week teaching at the Art Students League in New York, he savored the days he could devote to painting and gardening at his home in Greenwich. "I feel more and more contented with the isolation of country life," he wrote to J. Alden Weir on December 16, 1891. "To be isolated is a fine thing and we are then nearer to nature. I can see how necessary it is to live always in the country—at all seasons of the year."[5]

True to his word, Twachtman painted the brook that ran through his property throughout the year. His aim was not so much to investigate the diverse effects of light, as Monet had done, as to capture the nuances of nature's moods and his own. Scrutinizing Horseneck Falls from different viewpoints, under different weather conditions, he went beyond mere description to attain a Zen-like absorption in his subject. The high horizon line, close-up vantage point, and mesmerizing motion of the water in the present version of the scene intensify the sense of intimacy, as Twachtman leads the viewer through at least six shifts in the level and direction of the splashing, swirling, eddying stream.

1. The artist's son, J. Alden Twachtman, related this to John Douglass Hale; see Hale, "The Life and Creative Development of John H. Twachtman," P.h.D. dissertation, Ohio State University, 1957, p. 70

2. Carolyn C. Mase "John H. Twachtman," *International Studio* 72 (January 1921), p. lxxii

3. John C. Van Dyke, *Nature for Its Own Sake* (New York: Charles Scribner's Sons, 1898), p. 170.

4. Ibid., p. 169.

5. John H. Twachtman to J. Alden Weir, Weir Papers, Weir Farm National Historic Site, Wilton, Conn.; quoted in Dorothy Weir Young, *The Life and Letters of J. Alden Weir* (New Haven: Yale University Press, 1960; reprint, New York: Kennedy Graphics and DaCapo, 1971), pp. 189–90.

Winter at Portland, 1907

Oil on canvas, 25 × 30 inches
Gift of the Allen Tucker Memorial, 1966 (66.74.1)

Dubbed "the American Van Gogh" by contemporary critics, Allen Tucker made the transition from the Impressionism of his most revered teacher, John H. Twachtman, to European-inspired Expressionism.[1] Milton W. Brown wrote that of the artists identified as Impressionists after World War I, "only Allen Tucker, inspired by the violence of Van Gogh, offered something new in his crude but impassioned language of light."[2]

Tucker began his studies under Twachtman at New York's Art Students League. There, Twachtman taught Preparatory Antique, a required introductory course in which students made charcoal drawings from plaster casts of classical sculpture. Beginners were assigned to sketch fragments of hands and feet. Gradually given more difficult models, they were promoted to the next class as soon as they could make a competent drawing of a head or torso.[3] This system offered little opportunity for Twachtman to influence younger artists. That came, instead, during the summer classes in outdoor painting he offered in Cos Cob, Connecticut. Tucker joined the summer class in 1892, when Twachtman and J. Alden Weir shared the teaching. Ernest Lawson was, by Tucker's account, "the leading member of the class" that year, but "it was Twachtman who opened the door for me, and made me understand that . . . I didn't have to be like or unlike anyone else, . . . that the world was mine and that there was nothing between me and the wonder of it all but that rectangle of white canvas."[4]

Painted five years after Twachtman's death, *Winter at Portland* reveals his enduring influence on Tucker's palette and subject matter. The subdued, grayish tones recall those in such Twachtman oils as *Horseneck Falls* (no. 19). The winter landscape was closely identified with Twachtman, who had frequently depicted his Greenwich farm blanketed in snow. Although Tucker's subject was not his home ground, it was a place he knew well, the property of his friend Robert Hartshorne in Highlands, New Jersey, not far from Tucker's home in Locust Point. Although he was not an artist himself, Hartshorne frequently accompanied Tucker when he painted. Another token of their friendship is Tucker's full-length portrait of Hartshorne in evening clothes (location unknown). Since the seventeenth century, the Hartshorne family had lived on the estate they called Portland, overlooking the Navesink River in Monmouth County. When Tucker painted Portland, it was a working farm comprising about five hundred acres. The mansion commanded extensive river vistas, but, following Twachtman's example, Tucker chose an intimate view. The modest building that anchors his composition was Portland's powerhouse; the field behind it was a cow pasture.

Tucker's treatment of architecture in a natural setting recalls that of another of his teachers, Weir. As in Weir's *Connecticut Village* (no. 18), nature seems to shelter the man-made structures. Tucker organized his composition with rhythmic verticals, achieving pleasing variations in the tall, unequally spaced trees, the shorter, tightly linked uprights of the picket fence, and the more widely separated fence posts that divide foreground from middle ground. At lower left, a shrub rendered in calligraphic brushstrokes balances the blocky form of the powerhouse.

Tucker painted *Winter in Portland* near the end of his Impressionist period. In 1911 he joined with other progressive artists to form the American Association of Painters and Sculptors. Tucker was involved in the organization's major undertaking, the Armory Show, which in 1913 introduced modern European art to a large American audience. His own work was profoundly affected by the new European paintings he saw at the Armory Show, especially those by Vincent van Gogh. He adopted the dark contour lines and the juicy, heavily impastoed surface texture characteristic of the Dutch artist's works. Tucker taught at the Art Students League from 1921 to 1928. Just as Twachtman had introduced his students to Impressionism, Tucker encouraged their adoption of a painterly Post-Impressionism. His painting and his teaching helped lay the groundwork for American Modernism.

1. James W. Lane, "Vincent in America: Allen Tucker," *Art News* 38 (December 16, 1939), p. 13.
2. Milton W. Brown, *American Painting from the Armory Show to the Depression* (Princeton, N.J.: Princeton University Press, 1955), p. 81.
3. Spencer H. Coon, "The Work of the Art Students League of New York," *Metropolitan* 5 (June 1897), p. 424.
4. Allen Tucker, *John H. Twachtman,* American Artists Series (New York: Whitney Museum of American Art, 1931), pp. 7–8.

Windflowers, 1912
Oil on canvas, 30 × 36 inches
Rogers Fund, 1917 (17.36)

The subject of Donoho's painting is a native American wildflower, *Anemonella thalictroides,* commonly known as rue anemone or windflower. Growing wild in eastern woodlands or cultivated in shady gardens, the windflower blooms in May and June. Its slender stalks tremble in the slightest breeze, a characteristic that inspired its common name and that Donoho captured in the tangled mass of blossoms. Depicting the fragile, short-lived flowers, said to come and go with the wind, demands the spontaneous execution associated with Impressionism. (The painting was previously titled *Wind Flowers* because the artist misspelled the name, thereby emphasizing the expressive quality that the wind provoked.)

Earlier in his career, Donoho had favored the Barbizon painters' earthy palette and agrarian subject matter, such as sheep-dotted landscapes. A Mississippi native, he had fled with his widowed mother to Washington, D.C., during the Civil War. In 1878 he moved to New York to study at the Art Students League, where William Merritt Chase taught. The following autumn, he enrolled at the Académie Julian in Paris. During the next eight years, his fellow students there would include several artists in this exhibition: Frank W. Benson, Willard Metcalf, John H. Twachtman, Robert Vonnoh, and Edmund C. Tarbell. Donoho spent summers painting near the Forest of Fontainebleau, in the art colonies of Barbizon and Grez-sur-Loing. He began to exhibit Barbizon-style canvases at the Paris Salon in 1881 and in American exhibitions the following year. Childe Hassam credited Donoho's *La Marcellerie* (ca. 1882; Brooklyn Museum of Art), which he saw at the National Academy of Design in 1883, with inspiring him to enroll at the Académie Julian. It "was the best out-of-door picture painted by an American painter at that time," he declared later.[1]

Donoho returned to New York in 1887. Three years later, he settled in the remote Long Island township of East Hampton. There, a small group of well-established older artists gathered at the home of Thomas Moran, who was known for theatrical views of the American West. Donoho would prove to be an important figure in the art colony's conversion to Impressionism. In 1894, the year of his marriage to the former Matilda Ackley, he built an impressive Colonial Revival house on the edge of the village. Among the artist-friends who came to visit was Hassam, who rented the Donohos' carriage house beginning in 1898. (Three years after Ruger Donoho's death, his widow sold the cottage and a plot of land to the Hassams.)

Under Hassam's influence, Donoho adopted a modified Impressionist style. The lively brushwork, flickering sunlight, and high-keyed palette of *Windflowers* link it to the garden views that Hassam had been painting since early in his career. Donoho painted his own garden, the critic Royal Cortissoz wrote, "in the same spirit in which he pottered over its flowers and hedges, loving it all and understanding it."[2]

Windflowers may represent either the Donohos' property or the Woodhouse Gardens, a three-acre Japanese water garden fashioned from a swamp just across Egypt Lane from their East Hampton home. Hassam also painted at the Woodhouse Gardens. After Donoho's death, Hassam and J. Alden Weir selected *Windflowers* for the Metropolitan's collection.

1. Hassam interview (1927), De Witt McClellan Lockman Papers, Archives of American Art, Smithsonian Institution, Washington, D.C., roll 503; quoted in René Paul Barilleaux and Victoria J. Beck, *G. Ruger Donoho: A Painter's Path* (Jackson, Miss.: Mississippi Museum of Art, 1995), p. 32.

2. Royal Cortissoz, "An Artist Made Better Known Since His Death," *Tribune,* November 1916, Macbeth Gallery Papers, Archives of American Art, roll NMc2; quoted in Barilleaux and Beck, *Donoho,* p. 42.

Mayfair, 1913
Oil on canvas, 28 × 25⅜ inches
Purchase, Arthur Hoppock Hearn Fund, 1914 (14.72)

The subject of Mayfair is probably a garden party, or May fair, at the Beal family's forty-acre estate on the west bank of the Hudson at Newburgh, New York. In canvases like this, a contemporary critic wrote, Gifford Beal "peopled the country around Newburgh with ladies in crinoline and with the dandies of long ago."[1] The elegant strollers and splashing fountains recall Beal's paintings of Central Park, another of his favorite themes, and reveal the influence of his teacher, William Merritt Chase.

Beal began his artistic training at Chase's summer school at Shinnecock, Long Island, in 1892, when he was only thirteen. The boy's parents and sisters were traveling in Europe that summer, so he was sent to Chase's outdoor-painting sessions with his older brother, the painter Reynolds Beal. For the next nine years, Gifford Beal studied year-round with Chase, spending the summers at Shinnecock and taking weekly classes during the winters in Chase's famous Tenth Street studio. He continued his studies with Chase even during his four years at Princeton, from which he was graduated in 1900. From 1901 to 1903 Beal worked at the Art Students League under George B. Bridgman and Frank Vincent DuMond.

Beal first visited Europe on his honeymoon in 1908. He avoided Paris entirely, explaining later, "I didn't trust myself with the delightful life" there; "It all sounded so fascinating and easy and loose."[2] Partly because of this puritanical streak, and partly because Beal, unlike most of his contemporaries, eschewed European training, his friend Guy Pène du Bois called him "a link in the chain of our most characteristically national painters."[3]

Chase remained the dominant influence on Beal's career, less for any stylistic inspiration than for his attitude toward painting. "It was his enthusiasm and the spirit he could put into his pupils that made Chase a great instructor," Beal told an interviewer. Describing Chase, clad entirely in white except for a red boutonniere and giving his famous Monday-morning critiques at Shinnecock, Beal recalled that "by the time he got through talking to us . . . we were so crazy to get out and paint that half the time we would go without lunch."[4] Beal also credited Chase with gentrifying the profession of painting. The dapper Chase's impeccable dress set an example for his students, Beal maintained; "it made us respect him the more and, in turn, respect ourselves."[5] But while Chase was a dandy, Beal dressed as if he were a conservative banker.

Like his teacher, Beal often depicted scenes of upper-middle-class leisure. Unlike Chase, however, Beal was born into the privileged society he portrayed. From 1913 to 1920 he spent summers at the family's Newburgh estate, Wilellyn. There, he and his wife entertained friends, including Childe Hassam, and relatives, among them the artist's niece Marjorie and her husband, the collector Duncan Phillips. Mayfair depicts one such gathering. Women in pale dresses and men in elegant dark suits stroll in the shade of tall trees. A small white dog tugs at the leash held by a child. A woman, perhaps a nursemaid, pushes a pram shaded by a pink parasol. In Mayfair, Beal captured the untroubled effervescence of the years just before World War I—the period he called "the golden time when the world was at peace."[6]

1. Helen Comstock, "Gifford Beal's Versatility," International Studio 77 (June 1923), p. 236.

2. Gifford Beal, unpublished manuscript; quoted in Ronald G. Pisano and Ann C. Madonia, Gifford Beal: Picture-Maker, exhibition catalogue (New York: Kraushaar Galleries, 1993), unpaginated.

3. Guy Pène du Bois, "Paintings and Watercolors by Gifford Beal," Kraushaar Galleries, 1923; quoted in Gifford Beal 1879–1956, exhibition catalogue (New York: Kraushaar Galleries, 1979), unpaginated.

4. Richard Beer, "As They Are," Art News 32 (May 19, 1934), p. 11.

5. Gifford Beal, "Chase—the Teacher," Scribner's Magazine 61 (January 1917), p. 257.

6. Gifford Beal, unpublished manuscript; quoted in Pisano and Madonia, unpaginated.

23 JOHN SINGER SARGENT (1856–1925)

Mannikin in the Snow, ca. 1891–93

Oil on canvas, 25 × 30 inches
Gift of Mrs. Francis Ormond, 1950 (50.130.12)

Sargent painted *Mannikin in the Snow* in the company of his friend and fellow expatriate Edwin Austin Abbey. In the early 1890s Sargent and Abbey shared the lease of Morgan Hall, a country house in Fairford, Gloucestershire. There, over the course of several winters, the two of them painted in the huge studio that was built to accommodate their work on murals for the new Boston Public Library. Abbey had vouched for Sargent's ability to execute his first major public commission in a letter to the architect Charles F. McKim, writing that "the Boston people need not be afraid that [Sargent] will be eccentric or impressionistic, or anything that is not perfectly serious or non-experimental when it comes to work of this kind."[1]

Sargent traveled to Egypt, Greece, and Turkey to gather material for his wall and ceiling decorations tracing a history of religion. On his travels, he made detailed drawings of architecture, historical costumes, and people of diverse ethnic backgrounds. At Morgan Hall, he integrated his drawings into a coherent design to fit the library's vaulted spaces. Such accumulation of visual data was second nature to Abbey, whose reputation as an illustrator was based on his precise depictions of costume and setting, but the mammoth scale of his mural, *The Quest of the Holy Grail,* presented even him with formidable new challenges.

One day, as a diversion from their work on the murals, the two artists arranged a mannikin in the snow outside their studio and painted oil sketches of it from the window. The results perfectly reveal their dissimilar modes of seeing. Sargent made a record of what was before him: a lifeless dummy propped up in the unremarkable stable yard of a country house. Avoiding any artifice, he even included the stand whose base forms an inverted "V" on either side of the mannequin's feet. For Abbey, by contrast, the costumed figure inspired a medieval fantasy. Although Abbey's painting has not been located, the critic Royal Cortissoz described it as "the portrait of a living troubadour, wearing his cloak and feathered hat with an air and strumming his lute while he lustily sang."[2]

Possibly confusing Abbey's work with Sargent's, the latter's biographer Charles Merrill Mount mistakenly catalogued *Mannikin in the Snow* as *Pistol in the Snow (Illustration from Shakespeare's Henry V).*[3] Abbey had in fact depicted Pistol, a character in *The Merry Wives of Windsor, Henry IV,* and *Henry V,* in the illustrations of Shakespeare's plays that had occupied him since 1887. Sargent's only flirtations with Shakespearean themes were his portrayals of the famous actress Ellen Terry.[4] His *Ellen Terry As Lady Macbeth* (1889; Tate Britain, London) is "weird and wonderful," according to the Sargent scholars Richard Ormond and Elaine Kilmurray, "but, realist as he was, it characterizes the actress rather than her role."[5]

Sargent's commitment to visual reality was foreign to Abbey, who confided to a friend his ambivalence about his habit of living in the past: "looking at an old window . . . I don't see that window as it is," Abbey confessed, "but as it might have been, with the people whom it was made for and the people who made it looking through it at each other. Everything old I see that way. . . . I lose all the pleasure a modern should have in the real aspect of things, under the light."[6]

Depicting "the real aspect of things"—even so ordinary a thing as an artist's lay figure—Sargent demonstrated the Impressionist's devotion to subjects from everyday modern life. The vitality of his *Mannikin in the Snow* derives, not from any contrived historical narrative, but from his free and confident brushwork and the lively jolt of the crimson costume against the neutral background.

1. Quoted in E. V. Lucas, *Edwin Austin Abbey, Royal Academician: The Record of His Life and Work* (New York: Charles Scribner's Sons, 1921), vol. 1, pp. 231–32.

2. Royal Cortissoz, foreword to *The Edwin Austin Abbey Collection: Paintings, Drawings, and Pastels by Edwin Austin Abbey,* exhibition catalogue (New Haven: Gallery of Fine Arts, Yale University, 1939), p. 3.

3. Charles Merrill Mount, *John Singer Sargent: A Biography* (New York, W. W. Norton & Company, 1955; reprint, New York: Kraus Reprint Co., 1969), p. 467. Mount dates the painting 1889; however, based on Sargent's and Abbey's chronologies, the correct date is ca. 1891–93. I am grateful to Elaine Kilmurray and Marc Simpson for their opinions on the date.

4. Sargent painted three portraits of the actress, all titled *Ellen Terry As Lady Macbeth* (1889, Tate Britain, London; 1889, The National Trust, Ellen Terry Memorial Museum, Smallhythe, Kent; and 1906, after Sargent's sketch of 1889, National Portrait Gallery, London). Richard Ormond and Elaine Kilmurray, *John Singer Sargent: The Early Portraits* (New Haven and London: Yale University Press, 1998), pp. 186–90.

5. Ibid., p. 188.

6. Edwin Austin Abbey to Mary Gertrude Mead, ca. June 1889; quoted in Lucas, *Edwin Austin Abbey,* vol. 1, pp. 199–200.

24 WILLIAM DE LEFTWICH DODGE (1867–1935)

Venus in Atrium, 1908 or 1910
Oil on canvas, 39⅞ × 30 inches
Gift of Mr. and Mrs. Leftwich Dodge Kimbrough, 1972 (1972.192)

Venus in Atrium, painted in the artist's Long Island home, interweaves two contrasting threads in turn-of-the-century American art: the classicizing taste of the American Renaissance and the looser, brighter style of Impressionism.

Dodge's background and training cultivated the cosmopolitanism evident in this painting. In 1879, when he was twelve, his mother, an aspiring artist, took him and his two siblings to Europe. After a year in Munich, they moved to France, where Dodge would spend most of the next twenty years. He began his formal training when he was only fifteen, drawing from plaster casts at the Ecole des Beaux-Arts and working in the Académie Colarossi. After several years of preparation, he won admission to the Beaux Arts studio of Jean-Léon Gérôme, who was famous for crisply delineated renderings of mythological, historical, and orientalist subjects. Under Gérôme's tutelage, Dodge mastered academic figure drawing, a skill favored by the American civic leaders who would commission public murals from Dodge.

Dodge launched his career as a muralist in 1893 when he was invited to decorate the dome of the Administration Building at the World's Columbian Exposition in Chicago. The twenty-four-year-old artist's allegorical *Glorification of the Arts and Sciences* was admired by visitors to the fair and led to commissions to decorate such great public spaces as the Library of Congress, the New York State Capitol, and the Brooklyn Academy of Music.

While Dodge's reputation was based on his murals and his equally conservative large-scale exhibition pieces, he also produced more personal works in a markedly different style. His engagement with Impressionism intensified beginning in 1898, when he spent the first of three summers in Giverny. Often working in the garden of his close friend, the sculptor

and painter Frederick MacMonnies, Dodge concentrated on the theme of the nude in the open air that would become identified with the second generation of Americans in Giverny.[1] When he was not at Giverny, however, he continued to produce elaborate historical paintings for exhibition at the Salon. Dodge's return to the United States late in 1900 was marked by a solo exhibition in New York and Chicago. The mixture of academic and Impressionist pictures he displayed bewildered some critics, but one astutely noted that "it is all very European in spirit."[2]

That European spirit was also evident in the artist's country home. Dodge designed and built his Greek Revival mansion on a high bluff overlooking Smithtown Bay in Setauket, Long Island, in 1906. From the selection of the site to the construction and furnishing of the house, he kept the project secret from his wife until it was completed. Although Frances Pryor Dodge was angry at not having been consulted, she admired the results—including the mural of rose-garlanded cupids her husband painted on the ceiling of her boudoir. In honor of his wife, Dodge named the house the Villa Francesca.

A contemporary writer for the *New York Herald* described Villa Francesca as "a bit of ancient Greece set down on the shore of Long Island Sound."[3] Fluted Ionic columns spanned the façade, while a pair of caryatids copied from the Erectheum on the Acropolis in Athens supported a side porch. In the painting, one of the caryatids is visible just outside the window of the atrium. Although it was not open to the sky like its Roman prototype, the atrium was the most classical of the Villa Francesca's rooms. Its marble floor was bordered in a black-and-yellow mosaic in a Greek key pattern. In the center of the room a bronze cast of

MacMonnies's fountain figure *Pan of Rohallion* (1890) rose from a mosaic basin.

For *Venus in Atrium,* Dodge turned his back on the bronze to focus on a marble sculpture of a nude female torso bathed in the sunlight from the windows at the end of the room. He framed the torso obliquely between a tall column at the left and an oriental screen on the right. A Renaissance-style pedestal elevates the sculpture above a sun-dappled grouping of plants in containers. Dodge purchased the three-foot-tall statue in New York about 1904. The Dodge Venus, as it is called, is one of numerous versions of the so-called Medici Aphrodite, of which the most famous example is the Venus de Medici at the Uffizi Gallery in Florence. Inspired by the renowned nude statue by Praxiteles that stood in a sanctuary at Cnidos, the Medici Aphrodite has been copied extensively since the seventeenth century. The Dodge Venus may be either a Roman copy of the Greek original or an eighteenth- or nineteenth-century version made to meet the enormous demand for statues of this type.[4]

In depicting the sculpture, Dodge became a modern Pygmalion. A comparison of the painting and the actual sculpture, which belongs to the artist's grandson, reveals that the artist imbued the marble with flesh-and-blood sensuality. Ignoring the brownish streaks that flaw the white stone, he portrayed it with a lifelike blush. The curves of the painted figure, enhanced by backlighting, are more pronounced than those of the marble: the thighs, the abdomen, and, especially, the breasts are decidedly more voluptuous.

Venus in Atrium remained in the artist's family until they donated it to the Metropolitan. The sculpture has been exhibited widely in the South. In a recent exhibition of Dodge's work, it was installed beside the painting it inspired.[5]

1. William H. Gerdts, *Monet's Giverny: An Impressionist Colony* (New York: Abbeville Press, 1993), p. 149.

2. Georgia Fraser Arkell, "The Paintings of William de Leftwich Dodge," *Art Education,* February 1901, p. 242; quoted in Ronald G. Pisano, *William de Leftwich Dodge: Impressions Home and Abroad,* exhibition catalogue (New York: Beacon Hill Fine Art, 1998), p. 9. I am indebted to the latter source for biographical information on the artist.

3. Gustav Kobbé, "Ancient Greece Reproduced in Long Island Villa," *New York Herald,* August 14, 1910, magazine section, p. 11.

4. See Francis Haskell and Nicholas Penny, *Taste and the Antique* (New Haven: Yale University Press, 1981), pp. 325–28. I am grateful to Elizabeth Milleker of the Metropolitan's Department of Greek and Roman Art for information on the Medici Aphrodite.

5. The exhibition was held at Beacon Hill Fine Art in New York in 1998. See n. 2 for catalogue citation.

25 LOUIS KRONBERG (1872–1965)

The Pink Sash, 1913
Oil on canvas, 30⅛ × 22⅛ inches
Purchase, George A. Hearn Fund, 1913 (13.61)

Louis Kronberg is doubly represented in this exhibition: by his own painting, *The Pink Sash,* and in a portrait by his friend Arthur Clifton Goodwin, painted about the same time (no. 30). Little known today, Kronberg was born in Boston. He studied at the School of the Museum of Fine Arts, Boston, under Frank W. Benson and Edmund C. Tarbell, and at the Art Students League in New York. A scholarship enabled him to go to Paris, where, from 1894 to 1897, he studied at the Académie Julian under Jean-Joseph Benjamin-Constant and Jean-Paul Laurens. The major influences on Kronberg's work were Tarbell and the French Impressionist Edgar Degas, whom Kronberg emulated by decorating fans in the Japanese manner, making extensive use of the colored chalks called pastels, and, especially, by making dancers his thematic specialty.

Kronberg portrayed some famous performers, including the Russian ballerina Lydia Lopokova and the American choreographer and dancer Loie Fuller, whose dramatically lighted performances in free-flowing gossamer silk costumes also captivated the French Post-Impressionist Henri de Toulouse-Lautrec. Like Degas, however, Kronberg usually depicted anonymous members of the *corps de ballet* in unguarded moments backstage or in rehearsal. As Degas had done in such paintings as *The Ballet Class* (fig. 10), Kronberg sometimes contrasted the young dancers with older chaperones.

In *The Pink Sash* Kronberg differentiated the figures by means of color, costume, and pose. Dressed almost entirely in gray, the silver-haired woman is a shadowy foil to the brunette girl in a filmy white tutu, the pink color of whose sash and slippers is repeated in a blossom on the chair in the foreground. In contrast to the young dancer, whose head, back, arms, and legs are bare, the old woman's body is enveloped in heavy fabric that leaves only her face and hands exposed. As she stoops to tie the sash around the graceful ballerina's waist, the outline of her bent back forms one side of a triangle whose apex is the mirrored reflection of the younger woman's head. Viewed simultaneously from the front and the back, the dancer's head is set off from the neutral wall by the framed mirror and the soft hues of a reflected wall hanging.

The wide pink sash, the painting's focal point, is paraphrased by the floppy lavender ribbons on the old woman's hat, suggesting a link between the two figures that goes beyond their physical closeness. Is the elderly woman the ballerina's grandmother? Was she, too, a dancer? The former ballerina Teresa Cerutti-Simmons believed so. Describing Kronberg's *Visitor* (location unknown), which depicts the same older model intently observing a dancer practicing at the bar, she wrote: "The elderly lady who might well be the parent, or grandparent, of the 'star,' watches the exercises with that keen interest which shows that she, too, understands the game. [This juxtaposition] is a philosophic harmony which links the present to the past, for we all realize that this old lady once stretched her own once limber leg on that same bar."[1]

FIGURE 10
Edgar Degas, *The Ballet Class,* ca. 1880. Oil on canvas, 32⅜ × 30¼ inches. Philadelphia Museum of Art; Purchased with the W.P. Wilstach Fund

1. Teresa Cerutti-Simmons, "Behind the Scenes with Louis Kronberg," *American Magazine of Art* 19 (April 1928), p. 198.

J. ALDEN WEIR (1852–1919)

Fruit, ca. 1888

Oil on canvas, 21⅛ × 17³⁄₁₆ inches
Purchase, Gift of Robert E. Tod, by exchange, 1980 (1980.219)

This apparently artless arrangement of apples and tomatoes reveals the influence of two French painters: the eighteenth-century artist Jean Baptiste Siméon Chardin and the Impressionist Edouard Manet. Its modest subject matter and austere composition evoke Chardin while its dark tonality and fluid brushwork recall the still-life paintings that Manet created for his friends. The still-life genre, which engaged Weir throughout the 1880s, enabled him to consolidate earlier styles and move toward the Impressionism he adopted in the 1890s.

Weir's artistic training could be said to have begun at his birth. His father, Robert W. Weir, was a respected history painter and the professor of drawing at the United States Military Academy at West Point, New York. From an early age, J. Alden Weir frequented his father's studio, becoming as familiar with crayons and paints as he was with tops and kites. Under his father's tutelage, he learned to appreciate the old masters, including the Dutch still-life painters of the seventeenth century. The young Weir also benefited from the guidance of his older half-brother, the painter John Ferguson Weir, who would become the first director of the Yale School of Fine Arts.

After initial instruction from his father, J. Alden studied for three years at the National Academy of Design in New York. To complete his training, he sailed in 1873 for Paris; there, he spent four years in the studio of Jean-Léon Gérôme and three semesters as a matriculant in the Ecole des Beaux-Arts. Although he was in Paris at the time of the first Impressionist exhibitions, Weir preferred the academic styles of his French instructors. After visiting Manet's independent exhibition in 1876, he reported to his father that Manet's "value of color is not bad; this, however, is all I can say of him."[1] He had nothing good to say of the third Impressionist exhibition the following year. "I never in my life saw more horrible things," he wrote to his parents. "They do not observe drawing nor form but

give you an impression of what they call nature. It was worse than the Chamber of Horrors."[2]

Within a few years after his return to New York in 1877, however, Weir would develop a keen appreciation for the works of Manet and the Impressionists. During a visit to France in 1881, he purchased three canvases by Manet for the collector Erwin Davis and called on the artist at home.[3] Manet's influence began to appear in Weir's work, notably in the dark figure paintings and still lifes of the 1880s.

In the first half of that decade, Weir produced large-scale floral pieces, which found a ready market at a time when he sold little else.[4] Most were complex compositions crowded with multiple bouquets of mixed blossoms grouped with precious objects of ceramic or silver. While he continued to paint these salable canvases, Weir added a new type of still life to his repertoire in the mid-1880s. Smaller, simpler, and more intimate, these tended to feature fruit or kitchenware instead of opulent flowers and expensive antiques. An example of this later style, *Fruit* suggests why Weir was recognized as an American master of still life.

In a departure for him, Weir combined the tabletop and the hanging still-life formats in an arrangement more plausibly and typically employed in images of dead game. Here, a branch from an apple tree is suspended against a putty-colored wall; two more apples, a few leaves, and two tomatoes lie on a white tablecloth below. Like the *vanitas* paintings of the old masters, Weir's still life acknowledges the imperfections of nature. The apples are bruised and scarred; a fly has alighted on one, another fly crawls up the wall, and a third rests on the larger tomato. Quickly sketched, they achieve buggy three-dimensionality through their tiny shadows. From such humble components, Weir created an elegant decoration for the dining rooms of the Gilded Age. Its early owners included the important collectors Thomas B. Clarke and, later, Louisine and Henry Osborne Havemeyer.

1. J. Alden Weir to Robert Weir, Paris, April 24, 1876; quoted in Dorothy Weir Young, *The Life and Letters of J. Alden Weir* (New Haven: Yale University Press, 1960; reprint, New York: Kennedy Graphics and DaCapo, 1971), p. 96.
2. J. Alden Weir to his parents, Paris, April 15, 1877; quoted in ibid., p. 123.
3. Ibid., p. 145.
4. Ibid., p. 163.

27 EDMUND C. TARBELL (1862–1938)

Still Life: Vase of Peonies, ca. 1925
Oil on canvas, 21³⁄₁₆ × 25⅛ inches
Gift of Mrs. J. Augustus Barnard, 1979 (1979.490.1)

This appealing still life is one of several that Tarbell painted in the last decade of his life. After retiring in 1925 as director of the Corcoran School of Art in Washington, D.C., Tarbell settled with his family in New Castle, New Hampshire, the historic coastal village where they had summered since the turn of the century. In 1905 Tarbell had purchased a modest farmhouse to which he added a studio overlooking the Piscataqua River. For the rest of his life, he would often portray his family relaxing in their antique-filled country home. While still-life elements appear in the figural compositions and portraits on which his reputation was based, it was only in retirement that Tarbell turned his attention to the genre in its own right.

The peonies that grew in Tarbell's New Castle garden were his favorite still-life subject. He painted at least seven peony studies, usually depicting the lush flowers in Chinese porcelain containers and often adding statuettes, candlesticks, and other accessories. The Metropolitan's example is simpler than most. Tarbell painted out a figurine that he had included to the right of the bouquet, thereby enhancing the composition's pleasing asymmetry. The unadorned vase is placed off-center, the flowers and leaves are cropped at the left edge, and one long-stemmed blossom arches to the right, disguising the pentimento. Tarbell's loose brushwork perfectly captures the sumptuous abundance of the full-blown peonies. The neutral background and expressive brushwork of this still life recall works by the French painter Edouard Manet, which Tarbell may have seen during his student years in Paris or, later, in reproductions.

A vase similar to the one shown on this canvas, also filled with pink and white blossoms, appears in *Nude with Peonies* (1927; private collection) by Tarbell and his student Marguerite Stuber Pearson.[1] In that painting, a seated nude turns her head away from the viewer toward an arrangement of peonies, dramatically spotlighted against a dark background. The bouquet, positioned opposite the woman's head, appears to be a surrogate for another human figure: the blossoms face the woman, as if returning her gaze, and their soft pink and white petals echo the tones and texture of her skin. The sensuality that is merely suggested in the Metropolitan's still life is openly expressed in *Nude and Peonies*.

1. The painting is reproduced in Patricia Jobe Pierce, *Edmund C. Tarbell and the Boston School of Painting* (Hingham, Mass.: Pierce Galleries, 1980), following p. 126.

Bessie Potter, ca. 1895

Oil on canvas, 32 × 25⅝ inches
Bequest of Bessie Potter Vonnoh Keyes, 1954 (55.118)

The sculptor Bessie Potter Vonnoh (1872–1955) shared William Merritt Chase's devotion to subjects drawn from modern life. "What I wanted was to look for beauty in the every-day world," she explained, "to catch the joy and swing of modern American life."[1] Instead of designing grandiose public monuments, Potter specialized in creating small figurines of genteel women and children in contemporary dress.

Potter was born in St. Louis and raised in Chicago. Her father was killed in an accident when she was two years old. Shortly afterward, she succumbed to a mysterious malady that stunted her growth; as an adult, she would stand only four feet eight inches tall. By the time she recovered at age ten, Potter had developed strong self-discipline and sense of purpose. She enrolled at the School of the Art Institute of Chicago when she was fourteen. Lorado Taft, who had recently returned from three years of study at the Ecole des Beaux-Arts in Paris, had just been named the institute's first instructor of sculpture. He became the precocious teenager's mentor and a lifelong friend. As one of Taft's women apprentices, nicknamed the "White Rabbits," Potter modeled sculptural decorations for the World's Columbian Exposition, held in Chicago in 1893. Among the exhibits at the fair, she was intrigued with the statuettes by the Russian-born, Italian-based artist Paul Troubetskoy. Almost immediately, she adopted their diminutive scale and sketchy, impressionistic treatment for her own work.

Potter found further inspiration on a trip to Paris in 1895. She called on her hero, Auguste Rodin, and may have seen the popular domestic figural groups of Jules Dalou. Back in Chicago, she produced her best-known work, A Young Mother (1896; The Metropolitan Museum of Art). This study of a woman cradling an infant in her arms epitomizes the tender intimacy that typifies Potter's sculptures. Her work won the admiration of other artists as well as collectors. In a letter to a friend, the painter Theodore Robinson, who owned a Potter statuette, cited two qualities that appealed to the sculptor's patrons: "I like the little figures extremely," he wrote; "they are modern and feminine."[2]

At first, Chase's portrait of Potter appears to emphasize only her femininity while ignoring her professional activities. Her relaxed posture and elegant gown suggest that she is simply a wealthy young woman who could afford to commission a portrait from one of America's most famous painters. In fact, however, Potter's pose, costume, and hairstyle represent her deliberate construction of her artistic persona and Chase's complicity in recording it in his portrait of her.

Potter met the painter Robert Vonnoh at Lorado Taft's studio in 1892. They became close friends and married soon after the death of Vonnoh's first wife in 1899. By 1895 Vonnoh had painted the first of his three known portraits of Potter in the guise of the eighteenth-century French painter Elisabeth-Louise Vigée-Lebrun. The young sculptor seems to have delighted in the masquerade. While she was traveling in Italy in 1897, a Chicago paper reported, "Bessie Potter has been going to a fancy-dress party given by the Artists' Club of Florence, in the character of Madame Vigee-Lebrun [sic]. Long ago Mr. Vonnoh pointed out her resemblance to the famous French woman, and many of Miss Potter's friends possess her photograph taken in the costume and pose of one of Mme Lebrun's most charming self-portraits."[3]

Vigée-Lebrun was an appropriate professional ancestor for Potter. Enjoying the advantages of beauty, charm, determination, and an encouraging parent, she was one of the few eighteenth-century women artists to establish a successful career. Although Potter was not as beautiful as the French painter, she too was noted for a vivacious personality and unusual ambition, as well as for the sometimes obsessive devotion of her widowed mother. It may be more than a coincidence that Vigée-Lebrun's many self-portraits that portray her embracing one of her children anticipate the mother-and-child sculptures that were the childless Potter's most popular works.

Chase endorsed the Vigée-Lebrun persona in his portrait of Potter. The sculptor's white muslin turban with its flaring ties; curly, center-parted hair; seated position with head turned toward the viewer; and long-sleeved black dress were inspired by Vigée-Lebrun's self-portrait of 1790 in the Uffizi Gallery (fig. 11). Chase could have seen the self-portrait during his many trips to Florence or an engraving of it that was published in Vienna in 1804.[4] Vigée-Lebrun depicted herself as both a chic parisienne and a professional artist: palette and brushes in hand, she glances away from the canvas on her easel. While Chase did not depict Potter at work, his allusion to her famous predecessor suggested her position in the tradition of Western art. The reference was not lost on contemporary exhibition-goers. When Potter's portrait was shown at the Albright Gallery in Buffalo in 1906, one critic detected "a striking suggestion of the features of Madame Vigee Le Brun [sic], which nearly everyone remarks."[5]

Chase's portrait of Potter may have been painted in 1895, during the sculptor's visit to New York. Its sketchy quality suggests that work on it was interrupted when Potter left for Paris. The object in her hands resembles one of her sculptures, but it is so loosely painted it is impossible to be certain. Chase's strategy departs from that in his other portraits of women artists. He had his former student Dora Wheeler pose in an opulent Japanesque interior reminiscent of his own famous studios, though it may have been decorated by Wheeler herself (1883; The Cleveland Museum of Art). He depicted Annie Traquair Lang, another former student, as a fashionable young woman in a low-cut evening gown in a typical society-portrait composition (fig. 12). While Chase's portrait of Bessie Potter is much smaller and less finished than the life-size ones of Wheeler and Lang, it conveys greater respect for the sitter as a professional colleague. That admiration was well founded. Lang seems never to have emerged from her teacher's long shadow; Wheeler achieved distinction in the decorative arts, a field then considered inferior to the "fine arts" of painting and sculpture. Potter, on the other hand, had already established her professional niche by her mid-twenties, when she sat for her portrait by Chase.

1. Bessie Potter Vonnoh, "Tears and Laughter Caught in Bronze: A Great Woman Sculptor Recalls Her Trials and Triumphs," Delineator 107 (October 1925), p. 9.

2. Quoted in Julie Alane Aronson, "Bessie Potter Vonnoh (1872–1955) and Small Bronze Sculpture in America," Ph.D. diss., University of Delaware, 1995, p. 103. I am indebted to this source for biographical information on the sculptor and to Dr. Aronson for commenting on this catalogue entry.

3. Isabel McDougall, untitled clipping from the Chicago Evening Post, May 22, 1897, Art Institute of Chicago Scrapbooks, vol. 8, p. 129. I am grateful to Dr. Aronson for providing me with a photocopy of this clipping. None of the photographs mentioned in the newspaper account have been located.

4. The engraving is reproduced in Charles Pillet, Madame Vigée-Le Brun (Paris: Librairie de l'Art, 1890), p. 5.

5. "First Exhibition of Selected American Paintings at the Albright Gallery," Academy Notes 2 (June 1906), p. 20.

FIGURE 11
Elisabeth-Louise Vigée-Lebrun, *Self-Portrait*,
1790. Oil on canvas, 39⅜ × 31⅞ inches. Uffizi
Gallery, Florence

William Merritt Chase, ca. 1910

Oil on canvas, 30 × 25 inches
Gift of Mr. and Mrs. Raymond J. Horowitz, 1977 (1977.183.1)

Annie Lang was one of William Merritt Chase's star pupils, described by the master himself as "very gifted."[1] So successfully did she emulate his style that this work was exhibited, years after the deaths of both painters, as a self-portrait by Chase. Even one of Chase's daughters was fooled; believing that it was her father's self-portrait, she wrote, "It is the most striking likeness I have ever seen and made me feel very lonesome for him."[2]

Lang's debonair portrait of Chase was the product of long familiarity and close friendship. She attended his summer school at Shinnecock when she was only sixteen. By that time, she had already devoted several years to her artistic training. As a child, she took lessons in drawing, designing, wood-carving, and sculpture at the Public Industrial Art School in Philadelphia. A small portrait bust that she modeled when she was thirteen was cast in bronze by the city's leading sculptor, Albert Laessle. Lang won a scholarship to the Philadelphia School of Design for Women, where she continued her studies under William Sartain, Elliott Daingerfield, and Henry B. Snell. In 1906 she was awarded a scholarship to the Pennsylvania Academy of the Fine Arts, where she again worked under Chase as well as with Thomas Anshutz and Cecilia Beaux. Lang's debt to Beaux is evident in her elegant portrait of one of her earliest teachers, J. Liberty Tadd (undated; Pennsylvania Academy of the Fine Arts, Philadelphia).

Lang's promise was rewarded with scholarships to study in Europe in 1908 and 1910. While in Florence in 1910, she painted this portrait of Chase, who was conducting a summer session at a fifteenth-century villa overlooking the city. After a few seasons of renting the Villa Silli, Chase purchased it that summer, complete with some of its period furnishings.[3] The Florentine villa offered him an unprecedented opportunity to display antiques in a house as old as its contents, and he eagerly scoured the city's shops to augment its decoration. His colleague J. Carroll Beckwith, no doubt recalling Chase's famously cluttered Tenth Street studio, noted with relief after a visit to Villa Silli that "Chase had not yet got enough things to spoil it."[4]

The aesthetic interiors Chase had created in Shinnecock and New York had been the subject of many of his paintings. In that tradition, Annie Lang completed an impressive view of the Villa Silli's elegant salon (1910; location unknown). For the portrait, however, she posed Chase against a neutral dark background relieved only by the floral tapestry of his armchair. She depicted the dapper artist clad entirely in white, which complements his Van Dyck beard and handlebar mustache. A jeweled stickpin at his throat accentuates his ensemble. But in Lang's psychologically penetrating portrait, Chase is no mere dandy. As if he is impatient to resume work, his left arm is cocked back, ready to propel him from the chair. Eyes narrowed, he stares intently—perhaps evaluating the technique of his former student, perhaps gazing beyond her at a canvas of his own.

In this homage to her mentor, Lang adopted several characteristics of his work, thereby emulating the very pattern of stylistic emulation Chase had adopted when he painted James McNeill Whistler in Whistler's own style (1885; The Metropolitan Museum of Art). She appears to have worked quickly, as Chase urged his students to do. Her dashing, broad strokes with a loaded brush are especially evident in the white coat. A black ribbon unfurls from Chase's spectacles in a bold calligraphic line. The sketchy brushwork of his clothing compels closer attention to the subject's face; his piercing eyes are the focus of the composition.

After 1910 Lang visited Europe most summers, sometimes as a member of Chase's class, sometimes leading her own. In 1912 she painted a view of the aging artist at work in his studio in Bruges (location unknown). Chase in turn commemorated their friendship in at least three portraits of Lang. One, now in the Philadelphia Museum of Art, shows her as an alert, attractive young woman in a low-cut gown, seated on a velvet sofa (fig. 12).[5]

In 1917, the year after Chase's death, Lang had her first solo exhibition at New York's prestigious Knoedler Gallery. In a laudatory essay on Lang, the *International Studio* praised her "richness of colour, breadth and vigour of handling, [and] strong and piquant grasp of character," adding that her long study with Chase had "in no degree hampered her individuality."[6] That statement, which suggested that Lang might emerge from her teacher's shadow, was undermined by the news that her exhibition at Knoedler's was to be followed by one of her collection of Chase's works, then considered the finest in private hands. Just a year and a half later, Annie Lang died in the flu epidemic of 1918.[7] She was thirty-three. Some years later, her portrait of Chase was cut down from a slightly larger composition and a false W. M. Chase signature was added at the lower left.[8]

1. Guy Meredith, "Annie Traquair Lang," *International Studio* 61 (June 1917), p. cxvii. Most of the biographical information on Lang is based on this source.

2. Koto Chase Sullivan to Mrs. [Charles Finn] Williams, May 10, 1944, object file, Department of American Paintings and Sculpture, The Metropolitan Museum of Art.

3. Ronald G. Pisano, *A Leading Spirit in American Art: William Merritt Chase, 1848–1916,* exhibition catalogue (Seattle: Henry Art Gallery, 1983), pp. 138, 140.

4. Quoted in ibid., p. 138.

5. Guy Meredith's article on Lang (see n. 1 above) refers to two additional portraits of Lang by Chase (Meredith, p. cxviii). One of them is in a private collection; the location of the other is unknown.

6. Meredith, "Annie Traquair Lang," p. cxvii.

7. "Annie Traquair Lang," *International Studio* 66 (December 1918), supplement, p. 40.

8. The reattribution of the portrait was made by Pisano in the catalogue for Sotheby Parke-Bernet, December 12, 1975, lot 83.

FIGURE 12
William Merrit Chase, *Portrait of Annie Traquair Lang*, 1911. Oil on canvas, 59½ × 47¾ inches. Philadelphia Museum of Art; The Alex Simpson, Jr., Collection

Louis Kronberg in His Studio in Copley Hall, ca. 1913

Oil on canvas, 25¹/₁₆ × 21⅛ inches
Gift of Mr. and Mrs. Raymond J. Horowitz, 1975 (1975.397)

For the self-taught painter Arthur Clifton Goodwin, the Boston artist Louis Kronberg was mentor, benefactor, and friend. Goodwin was born in Portsmouth, New Hampshire, and grew up in Boston. In his late thirties, when he was working as a salesman for a wholesale paper company, he developed an interest in painting. He turned for advice to Kronberg, who was his junior by about eight years (see Kronberg's *The Pink Sash*, no. 25). One day about 1902, Kronberg recalled later, Goodwin appeared at his door saying that he admired his work and asked his help in launching a career as an artist. Although Goodwin admitted that he had never painted, Kronberg was impressed with his natural ability. He shared his studio and materials with him in 1903–4, and remained a close friend for the rest of his life. This generosity was the more remarkable because Goodwin abused alcohol, which resulted in wide fluctuations in his behavior and appearance.[1]

Goodwin, who never sought academic training and never traveled to Europe, achieved surprising success in his belated career. The art critics for Boston's *Daily Globe* and *Evening Transcript* praised his quickly executed canvases that portrayed the city's streets, docks, and markets. He exhibited at the Pennsylvania Academy of the Fine Arts, the Art Institute of Chicago, the Carnegie Institute, the National Academy of Design, and the Panama-Pacific International Exposition. He moved to New York in 1921 and married the following year. When, in 1929, Goodwin returned to Boston alone, Kronberg advised him to go to Paris to paint street scenes. After a bout of excessive drinking, Goodwin was found dead in his studio with his steamship ticket to France in his pocket.[2]

In this picture, Goodwin combined his self-portrait, reflected in the mirror, with that of his friend, shown at work in his studio in Boston's Copley Hall. The headquarters of the Copley Society, an artists' association, Copley Hall was the largest exhibition space in Boston at the time. It was located within the Grundmann

Studios, which had been converted from a roller-skating rink, but both the exhibition space and the studios were commonly called by the collective name Copley Hall.[3] From about 1911 to 1917, Kronberg, who taught a portrait class for the Copley Society, had a studio in the building. As Goodwin's painting reveals, the studio contained a patterned rug and a few pieces of furniture, which established an illusory domestic setting. The rough-hewn beams conjure up a romantic vision of an artist's garret.

Goodwin depicted Kronberg at work on a common American Impressionist motif: a woman doing needlework. William Merritt Chase explored the same theme in *For the Little One* (no. 35). The Boston Impressionists were even more closely identified with the subject, especially after 1905, when Edmund C. Tarbell's *Girl Crocheting* (fig. 13) was the sensation of the exhibition season. Kronberg had studied under Tarbell at the School of the Museum of Fine Arts, and the vignette he arranged in his studio seems to have been inspired directly by his former teacher's famous picture. In both paintings, light pours from a window behind a woman posed in left-facing profile, illuminating her neck, left shoulder, and arm, and silhouetting her against a neutral wall as she sits with head bowed over her needlework and hands held close to her face. While the genteel woman in a tasteful interior was Tarbell's signature theme, it was unusual in Kronberg's oeuvre. In Goodwin's canvas, the gauzy white tutu on the table beneath the mirror alludes to his mentor's more usual subject, the ballerina.

For Goodwin, too, the subject matter of this painting represents a departure. Until 1913 figures appeared only as minor elements in his urban landscapes. In a letter to the dealer William Macbeth dated July 28, 1913, he announced a shift in his emphasis: "I intend to go in for figure work with street, park, and other interesting backgrounds." In the same letter, he reported: "I am finishing a small canvas of Kronberg's studio

with him at work and his models posing reflected in the mirror the whole thing more or less novel."[4] While the painting may have been novel for Goodwin, it was decidedly old-fashioned, in comparison with the art that had been exhibited at Copley Hall a few months earlier. After showings at New York's Sixty-ninth Regiment Armory and the Art Institute of Chicago, the International Exhibition of Modern Art, more commonly called the Armory Show, was on view at Copley Hall from April 28 to May 19, 1913.[5] The works of such artists as Pablo Picasso, Georges Braque, Marcel Duchamp, Constantin Brancusi, and Henri Matisse bewildered many Bostonians. Two months after the exhibition closed, Goodwin depicted Kronberg painting a traditional subject in a style that had been rendered archaic by the bold new art that had recently been exhibited in the same building.

FIGURE 13
Edmund Charles Tarbell, *Girl Crocheting*, 1904. Oil on canvas, 30 × 26 inches. Canajoharie Library and Art Gallery, Canajoharie, New York

1. Lionello Venturi, *Arthur Clifton Goodwin*, exhibition catalogue (Andover, Mass.: Addison Gallery of American Art, 1946), p. 5. The biographical information in this entry is based on Venturi and two other exhibition catalogues: Sandra Emerson, Lucretia H. Giese, and Laura C. Luckey, *A. C. Goodwin, 1864–1929* (Boston: Museum of Fine Arts, 1974), and *An Exhibition of Oils and Pastels by Arthur C. Goodwin* (New York: Wildenstein Gallery, 1946).

2. Venturi, p. 8.

3. For information on the Grundmann Studios, I am grateful to Nancy Jarzombek, director of research, Vose Galleries, Boston. See also Trevor J. Fairbrother et al., *The Bostonians: Painters of an Elegant Age, 1870–1930*, exhibition catalogue (Boston: Museum of Fine Arts, 1986), p. 41, and Laura C. Luckey, "Goodwin in Context," in Emerson, Giese, and Luckey, *Goodwin*, unpaginated.

4. Arthur C. Goodwin to William Macbeth, July 28, 1913, Macbeth Papers, Archives of American Art, Smithsonian Institution, Washington, D.C., roll NMc7, frames 80–81.

5. See Milton W. Brown, *The Story of the Armory Show* (Greenwich, Conn.: New York Graphic Society, 1963), pp. 184–89.

Portrait of a Girl with Flowers, ca. 1913

Oil on canvas, 21 × 18 inches

Bequest of Miss Adelaide Milton de Groot (1876–1967), 1967 (67.187.137)

Prendergast's *Portrait of a Girl with Flowers* depicts Edith Lawrence King (1884–1975), an artist and teacher who was born in Boston and raised in Chelsea, a Boston suburb. Her father, Edwin, an importer, died young; her mother, Ellen Augusta Hough King, was a librarian at the Massachusetts Institute of Technology (MIT) in Cambridge. Edith King studied at the Rhode Island School of Design, the Women's College of Brown University, and informally with the sculptor Truman Bartlett at MIT.[1] She was teaching art at the Buckingham School in Cambridge when she met Maurice Prendergast and his brother Charles, who was also an artist. In the summer of 1911 Edith King, her mother, and her younger sister Marian vacationed on the Italian island of Capri. The Prendergast brothers were there at the same time, and Edith painted watercolors with Maurice. Although she was never his student (indeed, he had none), she was heavily influenced by the well-established older artist. The five watercolors she exhibited in the Armory Show of 1913, all of Italian subjects, reveal her debt to him.

The friendship seems to have had its ups and downs. When Maurice was hospitalized in Venice in the winter of 1911, he wrote to Charles, "I must say the women here are very fine, they are considerate and know all about sickness and misery—beside which the King girls are hard and crude."[2] Even Edith King's friends and relatives shared that harsh opinion of her personality. According to a later account, she "was known for her ruthless and brutally frank tongue, and used hysteria and migraine headaches to get her own way."[3] The

Prendergast scholar Nancy Mowll Mathews notes, however, that several of the twenty portraits Maurice Prendergast painted between 1910 and 1913 either certainly depict or strongly resemble Edith King. Among them is *La Rouge: Portrait of Miss Edith King* (ca. 1910–13; Lehigh University Art Galleries, Bethlehem, Pa.), in which the auburn-haired sitter wears the same amber necklace and nosegay as in the Metropolitan's canvas.

Further evidence of an enduring friendship is Charles Prendergast's involvement with the King-Coit School and Children's Theatre in New York. From 1923 to 1958 Edith King and her fellow teacher Dorothy Coit offered instruction in acting, dancing, drawing, and painting for children who came two afternoons a week at the end of their regular school day. Their pupils— who included the future dancers Tanaquil Le Clercq and Jacques D'Amboise; the actresses Jane Wyatt, Lee Remick, and Anne Baxter; and the writer Madeleine L'Engle—studied history, literature, and art in preparation for staging highly sophisticated plays. King-Coit's productions were reviewed in the *New Yorker, Saturday Review,* the *New York Times,* and other publications. Charles Prendergast served on the school's committee of sponsors (as did John Singer Sargent and George Bellows) and may have contributed to the set design of at least one of the plays.[4]

This portrait reflects the shift in Maurice Prendergast's style that followed his trip to France in 1907. (For his biography, see number 6.) He admired the work of the Fauves, Félix Valloton, Edouard Vuillard, and, especially, Paul Cézanne. Just before he left for home, he wrote to a friend, "I got what I came over for, a new impulse."[5] That new impulse is manifested in the distinctive brushwork of this canvas. Discrete strokes of a square, fairly wide brush unite flowers, background, and model's clothing in a decorative mosaic. The composition is structured around simple shapes: the circular volumes of face, hat, and pitcher; the inverted pyramid of the white collar; the rectilinear forms of picture frame and table. The square brushstrokes, geometric underpinning, and flattened space reveal the painter's debt to Cézanne.

Prendergast's modernist treatment of the time-honored theme of a woman with flowers contrasts with that of other American Impressionists. The paintings in this exhibition by Frederick C. Frieseke and F. Luis Mora, while very different from each other, both retain a naturalistic, three-dimensional modeling of the figure (nos. 33, 39). In Prendergast's canvas, on the other hand, only the model's face reflects the careful draftsmanship the artist had mastered years earlier in the Paris studios. The floral elements—the bouquet in the tall blue pitcher, the nosegay (possibly artificial) pinned low on the figure's bodice, the wreath of blossoms circling her broad-brimmed hat—lend an air of conventional femininity to the pretty model. Only her candid expression conveys the self-confidence that would enable Edith King to become an innovative, highly respected educator during a period when few women made their careers outside the home.

---

1. Biographical information on King is derived from Ellen Rodman, "Edith King and Dorothy Coit and the King-Coit School and Children's Theatre," Ph.D. diss., New York University, 1980, pp. 2–10.

2. Quoted in Nancy Mowll Mathews, *Maurice Prendergast,* exhibition catalogue (Williamstown, Mass.: Williams College Museum of Art, 1990), p. 30, n. 26. I am indebted to this source for biographical information on Prendergast.

3. Rodman, "Edith King," pp. 18 and 22.

4. Ross Anderson discusses the relation between the set of *Kai Khosru* (1924) and Charles Prendergast's work in his essay "Charles Prendergast," in Carol Clark, Nancy Mowll Mathews, and Gwendolyn Owens, *Maurice Brazil Prendergast, Charles Prendergast: A Catalogue Raisonné* (Williamstown, Mass.: Williams College Museum of Art; Munich: Prestel, 1990), pp. 91–92. Charles Prendergast's influence can also be detected in the sets of two other plays: *Aucassin and Nicolette* (1920; reproduced in Rodman, "Edith King," pp. vi and 150) and *Nala and Damayanti* (1922; reproduced in Rodman, "Edith King," p. 155).

5. Quoted in Mathews, *Prendergast,* p. 25.

American Impressionists Paint Domestic Life

Two Girls on a Lawn, ca. 1889

Oil on canvas, 21⅛ × 25¼ inches
Gift of Mrs. Francis Ormond, 1950 (50.130.40)

Two Girls on a Lawn compels attention with its bold graphic design, unusual vantage point, and limited palette. Two female figures recline on the bright green grass, their bodies merging into a languorous "S" composed of alternating blocks of black and white. Nestled together like spoons, they sprawl on the lawn as unselfconsciously as children. Their easy familiarity with each other is implicitly shared with the artist, who apparently sat at his easel while they lay at his feet. His spirited brushwork is most evident in the squiggles and dashes that describe the grass. The "whites" of hat and dress dissolve on closer inspection into luscious confections of cream, peach, turquoise, teal, blue, violet, pink—and white.

Sargent probably painted this canvas in the summer of 1889 at Fladbury Rectory, an old house he rented on the river Avon about ten miles from Broadway in Worcestershire, England. (For information on Sargent's visits to Broadway, see number 8.) His mother and his sisters, Emily and Violet, were with him in Fladbury, and they welcomed a houseful of guests, including the French painter Paul Helleu and his wife, Alice. Sargent's friends and relatives posed for numerous canvases that summer. *V & Katie Vickers* is inscribed in an unknown hand on the tacking edge of this canvas. "V" was presumably the artist's sister Violet, who was then nineteen. (In 1950, Violet Sargent Ormond donated to The Metropolitan Museum of Art this and many other paintings by Sargent, including all those in this exhibition.) In the painting, she wears a black dress because her father, Dr. FitzWilliam Sargent, had died a few months earlier. The woman in the white frock cannot be identified with certainty. Although Sargent portrayed several members of the Vickers family as early as 1882, no Katie Vickers is known. One art historian, probably unaware of the inscription, which is usually concealed by the frame of this painting, identified the model as Alice Helleu.[1] In any case, Sargent was concerned, not with capturing individual likenesses, but with creating a daring two-dimensional pattern. Since his sister would normally have worn a black bonnet to complete her mourning attire, he probably had his models exchange hats to produce a livelier play of black and white.

Many of Sargent's Fladbury paintings reveal the direct influence of the French Impressionist Claude Monet, whom Sargent had visited at his home in Giverny in 1885, in 1887, and possibly again in 1888.[2] *Two Girls on a Lawn,* however, relates more closely to the Japanese prints that Sargent, Monet, and other artists of the period so admired.

Two Girls on a Lawn is one of many images Sargent produced at Fladbury depicting well-dressed figures resting on the grass or in boats. Those paintings suggest the leisurely pace at the country retreat and convey the subtle eroticism that permeates much of Sargent's work. The art historian Trevor Fairbrother has traced Sargent's lifelong interest in the reclining figure, often in intertwined pairs or groups.[3] Three characteristics that Fairbrother observes in the artist's genre work— "languor and repose," "sensuality," and "dramatic presentation of the subject"[4]—combine to make this oil sketch a commanding presence even in a gallery of more finished paintings.

1. Warren Adelson, in Stanley Olson, Warren Adelson, and Richard Ormond, *Sargent at Broadway: The Impressionist Years,* exhibition catalogue (New York: Coe Kerr Gallery, 1986), pp. 53–54.

2. Richard Ormond and Elaine Kilmurray, *John Singer Sargent: The Early Portraits* (New Haven and London: Yale University Press, 1998), pp. 155–56.

3. Trevor Fairbrother, "Sargent's Genre Paintings and the Issues of Suppression and Privacy," *American Art Around 1900* (Washington, D.C.: National Gallery of Art, 1990), pp. 29–49.

4. Ibid., p. 30.

33 FREDERICK CARL FRIESEKE (1874–1939)

Woman with a Mirror (Femme qui se mire), 1911

Oil on canvas, 31⅞ × 32 inches
Gift of Rodman Wanamaker, 1912 (12.42)

Frederick Carl Frieseke painted *Woman with a Mirror* in Giverny, France, where he lived from 1906 to 1920 near Claude Monet in a house once occupied by Theodore Robinson. Just as Robinson had been the most prominent of the first generation of American artists in Giverny, Frieseke was the leader of the group who congregated there in the first two decades of the twentieth century.[1] Unlike Robinson, however, Frieseke did not enjoy a close friendship with Monet, nor did he choose the local landscapes and people as his subjects. Instead, Frieseke initiated the focus on the theme with which the so-called Giverny Luminists would become identified: women in the boudoir or garden, either fashionably dressed or nude.

Frieseke arrived in Giverny via the standard path of American artists of his period: early training in the United States, followed by study in Paris. Despite his claim that he was essentially self-taught, Frieseke's professional preparation was extensive. He enrolled at the School of the Art Institute of Chicago in 1893. Three years later, he moved to New York, where he studied at the Art Students League. In 1898 the twenty-four-year-old artist sailed for France, where he would spend the rest of his life. James McNeill Whistler had just opened the Académie Carmen in Paris, and Frieseke studied briefly there under the older expatriate. He also enrolled at the Académie Julian, where his classmates included Richard E. Miller, who would later be a neighbor in Giverny.

Like other art students of the period, Frieseke developed his skill in plein-air painting during summers in art colonies. He first visited Giverny in 1900 but spent the following summer at Le Pouldu in Brittany. After he had completed his training, he returned to Giverny in 1906 with his wife, the former Sarah O'Bryan, and rented a cottage next door to Monet. The Friesekes eventually bought the house. Although they maintained an apartment in Paris, they made Giverny their primary residence until 1920, when they moved to another town in Normandy.

Not surprisingly, the influences on Frieseke's art were overwhelmingly French. The sugary palette, playfully erotic subject matter, and delight in feminine finery demonstrate his susceptibility to the eighteenth-century rococo painters Antoine Watteau and Jean-Honoré Fragonard. His models invoke Pierre-Auguste Renoir's monumental, full-figured nudes, and his fascination with pattern reveals his debt to his contemporaries, the Post-Impressionists Pierre Bonnard and Edouard Vuillard. In *Woman with a Mirror,* he used the large looking glass to carry the floral designs of the bouquet and the chintz from the foreground deep into the pictorial space. He structured this play of soft-edged patterns within a geometric framework of repeated verticals and horizontals.

Frieseke told an interviewer in 1914 that he lived in France because "there are not the Puritanical restrictions which prevail in America. . . . I can paint a nude in my garden or down by the fish pond and not be run out of town."[2] The overt eroticism that troubled many of Frieseke's American contemporaries is apparent in *Woman with a Mirror.* While the theme of a fashionable woman at her dressing table was shared by other American Impressionists, including Mary Cassatt and Childe Hassam, Frieseke's treatment was distinguished from theirs by its frank sensuality. Cassatt's and Hassam's models were usually garbed modestly in kimonos or dressing gowns, but Frieseke's wears only a chemise, corset, and petticoat. The voyeuristic effect of the low vantage point is heightened in a provocative game of display and concealment. The woman's raised arm reveals her breast while partially hiding it. In the mirrored image, the bouquet covers one breast while a strategically placed blossom directs attention to the other. The woman languidly dangles a stylish Eastern-inspired necklace, which frames her exposed breast and brushes her nipple, visible just above the mirror's edge. The intimacy of the boudoir is heightened by the reflected bed hangings.

Frieseke's affinity for French art won him critical success in his adopted country. Reviewing the Salon of 1904, from which the French government purchased a similar painting by Frieseke, a reporter for a Paris periodical wrote approvingly that the American's work was "impregnated" with French art. The New York dealer Robert Macbeth did not consider it a positive influence, however. After years of trying with limited success to sell works like *Woman with a Mirror,* he complained in 1919 that they were "perhaps a bit 'Frenchy' for the American buying public."[3]

1. For more on the art colony, see William H. Gerdts, *Monet's Giverny: An Impressionist Colony* (New York: Abbeville Press, 1993).

2. Clara T. MacChesney, "Frieseke Tells Some of the Secrets of His Art," *New York Times,* June 7, 1914, section 6, p. 7.

3. Robert Macbeth to Frieseke, July 2, 1919, Macbeth Gallery Papers, Archives of American Art, Smithsonian Institution, Washington, D.C., roll McB46, frame 275.

Across the Room, ca. 1899

Oil on canvas, 25 × 30⅛ inches
Bequest of Miss Adelaide Milton de Groot (1876–1967), 1967 (67.187.141)

This painting has been called *The White Dress, The Leisure Hour, By the Window,* and *Across the Room,* but one critic considered a different title the obvious choice. "It might just as well have been called 'The Studio Floor,'" he wrote when the painting was first exhibited in 1899, "for three-quarters of the picture represented its polished surface, reflecting a little light that came in between the closed slats of the blind."[1]

The unorthodox composition to which that critic objected reveals Tarbell's debt to the French Impressionist Edgar Degas and the American expatriate artist James McNeill Whistler. Tarbell expressed his enthusiasm for both painters in his comments on the art exhibitions at the World's Columbian Exposition, held in Chicago in 1893. "Nothing else in the whole show can be compared to [a] wonderful masterpiece of Degas's," he enthused, referring to *The Ballet Class* (fig. 10, p. 88). Tarbell described the picture of an odd little woman in the foreground reading a newspaper while a dance master coaches three young ballerinas who are squeezed into the upper left corner of the canvas. "The persons are not interesting nor good looking," Tarbell explained. Instead, "the way this thing is painted" won his admiration.[2] In *Across the Room,* Tarbell employed some of the same devices Degas had used. He organized his composition around diagonals and rectangles, pushed an important visual element to the top of the canvas, filled a large portion of the image with empty floor, and created a play of reflections with light from a window.

Similar strategies appear in a landscape by Whistler that Tarbell admired at the Chicago fair. In *Nocturne in Blue and Gold: Valparaiso* (fig. 14), the bold diagonal of a darkened wharf dominates the lower half of the canvas, while the indistinct forms of sailing ships, their lanterns shimmering on the water, are pushed to the top. In the upper left, fireworks burst against the night sky. The effect of the reflections was, Tarbell declared, "marvelous."[3]

Degas, Whistler, and Tarbell were all indebted to Japanese art for their asymmetrical compositions and daring use of empty space. In *Across the Room,* the Chinese porcelain jar and Japanese screen further demonstrate Tarbell's esteem for Asian art. Such objects served a dual role for Tarbell and his fellow Bostonians: they indicated the owner's sophisticated taste and they suggested a link with the China trade that was an essential part of New England's history. A more important status symbol in Tarbell's painting, however, was the woman lounging on the Sheraton sofa. In his influential *Theory of the Leisure Class,* published in 1899—about the time Tarbell painted this picture—Thorstein Veblen conjectured that a wealthy woman was expected to display her husband's or father's status through her unproductive idleness. Such a woman, Veblen wrote, "is exempted, or debarred, from vulgarly useful employ—in order to perform leisure vicariously for the good repute of her natural (pecuniary) guardian."[4]

The subject of a woman doing nothing, or nothing much, in a genteel home became identified with the Boston Impressionists. Tarbell, Frank W. Benson, Philip L. Hale, Joseph DeCamp, and William MacGregor Paxton were the best known of a group of painters who specialized in portrayals of such idle upper-middle-class women in airless, if elegant, interiors. These painters' designation as "Tarbellites" reflects Tarbell's position of leadership. Most of the Boston Impressionists were affiliated with the School of the Museum of Fine Arts in that city. Tarbell, who was born in West Groton, Massachusetts, and reared in Dorchester and South Boston, studied at the newly formed Museum School from 1879 until about 1882. There he began a lifelong friendship with Frank Benson, with whom he also studied at the Académie Julian in Paris from 1884 to 1886. Back in Boston, Tarbell and Benson joined the Museum School faculty in 1889, where both continued to teach until 1913. (Benson was a visiting instructor for another four years.) In that position, Tarbell influenced a generation of Boston artists.

Across the Room, a transitional work in Tarbell's oeuvre, was painted between the two periods of his mature career. During the 1890s, he attracted critical and popular acclaim for brightly colored, sunny figural

FIGURE 14
James McNeill Whistler, *Nocturne in Blue and Gold: Valparaiso,* 1866. Oil on canvas, 29¾ × 19¾ inches. Freer Gallery of Art, Smithsonian Institution, Washington D.C.

landscapes that manifest his fullest assimilation of French Impressionism. Between about 1903 and 1914 he shifted to darker tonalities and a more subdued atmosphere in images of solitary women in dimly lit interiors. The works of that period, including *Girl Crocheting* (fig. 13, p. 98), reveal the influence of the seventeenth-century Dutch painter Jan Vermeer. The sketchy brushwork and bold composition of *Across the Room* link it to Tarbell's earlier excursions into Impressionism, but its filtered light and muted palette ally it to the works inspired by Vermeer.

1. Charles H. Caffin, ed., "Ten American Painters," *Artist* 25 (May–June 1899), p. vii. This review is devoted to the second exhibition of the group known as the Ten.

2. "A Boston Artist's Comments on the Art Galleries of the World's Fair," *Boston Evening Transcript,* May 26, 1893, clipping, artist's file, Department of American Paintings and Sculpture, The Metropolitan Museum of Art.

3. Ibid.

4. Quoted in Patricia Hills, *The Painters' America: Rural and Urban Life, 1810–1910* (New York: Praeger Publishers, 1974), pp. 97 and 106.

For the Little One, ca. 1896

Oil on canvas, 40 × 35¼ inches
Amelia B. Lazarus Fund, by exchange, 1917 (13.90)

For the Little One depicts the artist's wife, Alice Gerson Chase, sewing in their summer house in Shinnecock, Long Island. The Chases were married in 1887, when he was thirty-eight and she was twenty-one. They had thirteen children, of whom eight survived infancy.[1] The "little one" of the title was probably their fifth child, Helen Velasquez, who was born in the Chases' New York home in 1895. At Shinnecock two years earlier, her parents had announced the birth of another daughter, Hazel, by flying a Japanese textile fish from the rooftop. Hazel was deemed "the first white child born on Shinnecock Hills, which were formerly occupied by the Indians. For that reason the child was given an Indian middle name, Neamaug, meaning 'between two waters,' which perfectly describes the location of the Chase house."[2]

Shinnecock Hills is part of the town of Southampton on Long Island's south fork. There, at the invitation and with the support of a group of prominent local residents, Chase conducted classes in outdoor painting from 1891 to 1902. The Shinnecock Hills Summer Art School, the largest and most famous of its kind in the United States, attracted about one hundred students each year. They lived in the Art Village, a cluster of cottages surrounding a large studio building. Chase's home, designed by his friend Stanford White, was located several miles from the Art Village. Chase taught on Mondays and Tuesdays, devoting the rest of the week to his own work. The canvases he created at Shinnecock have been called "the most lovely, most moving, and most assured works that Chase ever made."[3]

Chase's Shinnecock images fall into two broad categories: landscapes and interiors. The landscapes show the beaches and dunes near the Chase home, often populated by Mrs. Chase and their children; the interiors depict the family in the refined setting of their summer home. In *For the Little One,* Chase employed the graduated rectangles of pictures, window, and breakfront to establish a geometric structure for his composition. Each of those rectangles offers a glimpse of something within or beyond, revealing an aspect of Chase's life or art. The sheer-curtained window frames a section of the white porch railing and the grass-covered dunes. The breakfront's glass-enclosed bookcase is the window's physical and metaphorical twin, suggesting the reflective, interior life as contrasted with the active, outdoor life implied by the landscape. Just as Chase paired the window and the bookcase, he also paired two images of his wife, intimating the public and private realms. The unframed picture suspended from the window frame appears to be a portrait of Mrs. Chase wearing dark city garb, in contrast to the pale, summery frock she wears in her country home. While the urban woman's gaze is directed outward, the seated woman, sheltered in her country home, is absorbed in her sewing.[4]

Chase depicted his home as a genteel retreat presided over by his wife. He conveyed its calm atmosphere with a palette of harmonious warm neutrals, in which touches of red—Mrs. Chase's tiny slippers, her sewing basket, a book in the breakfront—inject a note of gaiety. Swaths of white, suggesting purity and innocence, surround the female figure. This domestic Madonna holds her needlework, implicitly intended for a "little one," in the position that would be occupied by a child.

Chase arrived at the Impressionist palette and concern with light manifested in *For the Little One* after passing through several other artistic phases. Born in Indiana, he went to New York in 1869 for two years of study at the National Academy of Design. In 1872 he left for Munich, where he spent six years as a student at the Royal Academy and in the circle of the Munich Realist Wilhelm Leibl. There, he adopted Leibl's expressive brushwork and dark palette, influenced by the seventeenth-century Dutch and Spanish masters. Unlike his classmate John H. Twachtman, Chase did not seek to undo his Munich tendencies through training in Paris. Instead, he gradually revised his art during the 1880s, prompted by the contemporary Belgian painter Alfred Stevens. "Don't try to make your pictures look as if they had been done by the old masters," Stevens cautioned Chase. "I saw the truth of his remark," Chase recalled later, adding, "modern conditions and trends of thought demand modern art for their expression."[5] In seeking to reconcile the lessons of the past with the flavor of the present, Chase took Diego Velázquez as a model. Like nineteenth-century American artists, Velázquez had studied abroad, Chase explained, but after emulating past masters, the Spanish painter had chosen "new forms and arrangements, new schemes of color and methods of painting, to fit the time and place he was called on to depict."[6] In his self-revision, Chase drew on varied sources: the French Impressionist paintings he saw on his travels and in Durand-Ruel's New York gallery; James McNeill Whistler, whose delicate, understated works Chase admired; the pastel medium, which fostered a lightness of touch and palette; and Japanese woodblock prints, whose asymmetrical compositions, bright colors, and bold use of empty space profoundly affected Chase and many of his contemporaries.

In a series of paintings of New York's Central Park and Brooklyn's Prospect Park done in the late 1880s, Chase developed a fresh, modern style, which culminated in his Shinnecock landscapes and interiors of the 1890s. He did not entirely abandon the lessons he had learned from his predecessors, however. Instead, borrowing from old and new, East and West, he created a composite, Americanized version of Impressionism. "The great record of America must come from Americans themselves," Chase told an interviewer.[7] In paintings like *For the Little One,* he left a compelling record of upper-middle-class American life at the turn of the last century.

1. Ronald G. Pisano, *A Leading Spirit in American Art: William Merritt Chase, 1849–1916,* exhibition catalogue (Seattle: Henry Art Gallery, University of Washington, 1983), pp. 46 and 188, n. 53.

2. Katharine Metcalf Roof, *The Life and Art of William Merritt Chase* (New York: Charles Scribner's Sons, 1917), p. 185.

3. D. Scott Atkinson and Nicolai Cikovsky, Jr., *William Merritt Chase: Summers at Shinnecock, 1891–1902,* exhibition catalogue (Washington, D.C.: National Gallery of Art, 1987), p. 10.

4. For this insight about the picture within the picture, I am indebted to H. Barbara Weinberg, Doreen Bolger, and David Park Curry, *American Impressionism and Realism: The Painting of Modern Life, 1885–1915,* exhibition catalogue (New York: The Metropolitan Museum of Art, 1994), p. 115.

5. "The Import of Art. By William M. Chase. An Interview with Walter Pach," *Outlook* 95 (June 25, 1910), p. 442.

6. Ibid. Diego Velázquez (1599–1660) went to Italy in August 1629 to study Italian painting and classical sculpture, returning to Madrid in December 1630.

7. Ibid.

Spring: Margot Standing in a Garden (Fillette dans un jardin), 1900

Oil on canvas, 26¾ × 22¾ inches
Bequest of Ruth Alms Barnard, 1982 (1982.119.2)

Mary Cassatt's *Spring: Margot Standing in a Garden* is one of the most beloved paintings in the Metropolitan's American Wing. Visitors gravitate to the canvas; many can be overheard declaring it their favorite. What is the source of this immense popular appeal?

The most obvious answer is that the subject is undeniably cute. Cassatt's model, Margot Lux, lived in the village near the artist's country home, the château de Beaufresne, at Mesnil-Théribus, on the Oise river. Cassatt made at least four dozen oils, pastels, and drawings of Margot. In all of those images, but especially in *Spring,* the young model's physical allure is apparent. Skirting the edge of sentimentality, Cassatt conveyed Margot's childish charm in rounded shapes: her cushiony bonnet, big brown eyes, dimpled cheeks, bare shoulder, puffed sleeves, and chubby arms and hands are echoed by curves in the landscape. Unctuous brushwork renders the soft textures of downy flesh, luscious velvet, and filmy pinafore.

We view Margot from child height, like a loving relative crouched before her, but she eludes our gaze. Her indifference to an adult presence suggests the idealized innocence that the art historian Anne Higonnet defines as characteristic of "the Romantic child." According to Higonnet, "the image of the Romantic child is an unconscious one, one that does not connect with adults, one that seems unaware of adults." She describes another painting of a little girl, Sir Joshua Reynolds's *Portrait of Penelope Boothby* (1788; Ashmolean Museum, Oxford), in terms that apply equally to Cassatt's *Spring:* "The child . . . is presented for us to look at, and to enjoy looking at, but not for us to make any psychological connection with. She glances . . . aside; she is absorbed in childhood."[1]

Cassatt emphasized the ideal of innocence by posing the child in a garden and linking her coloristically to nature. The white-trunked sapling with its bright red fruit is echoed in Margot's white pinafore, currant-colored dress, and auburn hair, while taller trees in the distance repeat the hue of her spruce-green bonnet. The milliner's flower on Margot's hat is obviously artificial; the child herself, the painting implies, is the real blossom in this garden. Cassatt's contemporaries readily understood her visual language, as evidenced by the caption when *Spring* was reproduced in *Good Housekeeping* in 1914: "Like a flashing flower, unconscious part of the garden itself, is this little bright-eyed maid."[2]

The ideal of childhood innocence encoded so skillfully in Cassatt's painting veils an element of sensuality. Margot's fashionable costume is slightly too large for her. The amusingly oversized hat emphasizes her small size and physical vulnerability. The dress and pinafore slip from her shoulder to expose her plump little shoulder and chest. By extending the curve of Margot's drooping neckline in the swing of the road behind her, Cassatt calls attention to her décolletage. The uneasy sense that Margot is about to shed her clothing is heightened by her childish gesture of clutching her pinafore. Tension arises from the disparity between the child's innocence and the adult's knowledge; between the little girl's unconsciousness of her disarrayed attire and the adult's awareness of exposed flesh. The child inhabits Eden before the Fall; the adult scrambles to find a fig leaf.

If viewers today are alert to such psychosexual meanings, Cassatt's contemporaries were at least dimly aware of them. When the canvas was exhibited at the St. Botolph Club in Boston in 1909, the painter and critic Philip L. Hale commented, "the kid [in *Spring*] is an amusing little wretch, quite Gallic in character."[3] To Americans then, "Gallic" denoted an enjoyment of sensual pleasures decidedly foreign to the descendants of the Puritans.

By the time Cassatt created this engaging picture, she was known primarily as a painter of mothers and children. That theme dominated her work only after about 1895, however. Earlier in her career, she had explored a wide range of subjects drawn from her life as an upper-class American expatriate in Europe. Cassatt was born in Allegheny City, Pennsylvania (now part of Pittsburgh), and grew up in Philadelphia and in France and Germany, where her wealthy family lived between 1850 and 1855. Back in the United States, she studied at the Pennsylvania Academy of the Fine Arts from 1860 to 1865. She persuaded her parents to let her complete her studies abroad and sailed for Paris late in 1865. She studied under Jean-Léon Gérôme and Charles Chaplin in Paris, and with Edouard Frère, Paul Soyer, and Thomas Couture in the French countryside. One of her paintings was accepted for the annual Salon for the first time in 1868, marking her debut as a professional artist. The outbreak of the Franco-Prussian War forced her to return to Philadelphia in 1870, but the following year she sailed for Italy with her artist-friend Emily Sartain. Cassatt traveled in Spain, Italy, Belgium, Holland, and France to study and copy the old masters. She returned to Paris in 1873 and made it her principal base for the rest of her life (she would also work at country houses, the last of them the château de Beaufresne).

While strolling through the Salon in 1874, Degas, who had not yet met the American artist, stopped before Cassatt's entry and remarked to a friend, "This is someone who feels as I do."[4] Three years later, when one of Cassatt's paintings was rejected by the Salon jury, Degas urged her never to submit anything to the Salon again and invited her to exhibit with the Impressionists. "I agreed gladly," she later told her first biographer, Achille Segard. "At last, I could work absolutely independently, without worrying about the possible opinion of a jury! I had already acknowledged who my true masters were. I admired Manet, Courbet, and Degas. I hated conventional art."[5] The only American formally associated with the Impressionists, Cassatt participated in four of their eight exhibitions. Degas was a close friend and mentor who, like Cassatt, concentrated on figure compositions rather than landscapes. Many of Cassatt's paintings, including *Spring: Margot Standing in a Garden,* also reveal close affinities with those of Pierre-Auguste Renoir.

1. Anne Higonnet, *Pictures of Innocence: The History and Crisis of Ideal Childhood* (London and New York: Thames and Hudson, 1998), p. 28.

2. Elisabeth Luther Cary, "Painting Health and Sanity," *Good Housekeeping* 58 (February 1914), p. 155.

3. Philip L. Hale, [review of Cassatt's St. Botolph Club exhibition], *Boston Herald,* February 8, 1909, p. 3, clipping, courtesy Boston Public Library.

4. Achille Segard, *Un Peintre des enfants et des mères, Mary Cassatt* (Paris: Librairie Paul Ollendorf, 1913), as excerpted in Nancy Mowll Mathews, *Cassatt: A Retrospective* (Southport, Conn.: Hugh Lauter Levin Associates, 1996), p. 100. The painting was *Ida* (reproduced in Nancy Mowll Mathews, *Mary Cassatt: A Life* [New York: Villard Books, 1994], p. 91).

5. Mathews, *Cassatt: A Retrospective,* p. 100.

MARY CASSATT (1844–1926)

Portrait of a Young Girl, 1899

Oil on canvas, 29 × 24⅛ inches
From the Collection of James Stillman, Gift of Dr. Ernest G. Stillman, 1922 (22.16.18)

One of the characteristics that distinguished Mary Cassatt from her artist-contemporaries was her commitment to exploring all the phases in the life of a modern woman. While other late-nineteenth- and early-twentieth-century artists, especially men, tended to limit their subjects to beautiful young women, Cassatt created psychologically perceptive images of her gender from early childhood, as in *Spring: Margot Standing in a Garden* (no. 36), through adolescence and the various stages of maturity to old age. In this aptly titled *Portrait of a Young Girl,* the model (whose identity is unknown) is poised between childhood and adulthood. Cassatt's early biographer, Achille Segard, believed that the model was about seventeen or eighteen, though to our eyes she appears younger.[1] She is dressed in the height of Belle Epoque fashion, but seems unconscious of her stylish costume. Absorbed in her own thoughts, she holds a blade of grass between her fingers and her lips. That childish gesture subverts the sophistication of her dress and heightens the sense of time's passage. Stretched to the breaking point, the grass will soon snap, recalling the girl from her reverie and prompting her, perhaps, to assume an ingratiating public face.

Cassatt used a variety of formal means to create this compelling portrait of a pensive adolescent. By choosing a close-up vantage point and obliterating the horizon line, she concentrated attention on the subject's head, which occupies the exact center of the composition. The artist established a conventionally "feminine" mood with a preponderance of curving lines and rounded forms, not only in the model's costume, face, and figure but also in the arcs of the driveway and the soft mounds of the shrubbery. In sharp contrast with those curves is the straight, taut blade of grass, which confirms her tie to the natural world. Already immersed in nature—the girl's head is below the horizon line and she is surrounded by the lush green meadow—she literally consumes it in a primitive communion.

Cassatt may also have used symbols to enrich the emotional content of this image of a girl on the brink of womanhood. During the 1890s, her studies of modern women took on larger, spiritual meanings characteristic of the contemporary movement called Symbolism.[2] In her murals (now lost) for the 1893 World's Columbian Exposition in Chicago, for example, she used symbolic imagery to depict *Young Women Plucking the Fruits of Knowledge* and *Young Women Pursuing Fame*. In *Portrait of a Young Girl,* the road—a traditional symbol of life—is mostly hidden: the way is unclear; the destination, like the girl's future, is unknown. Cassatt rendered the driveway in two bold half-moons whose prominence feeds the suspicion that she intended them to be read metaphorically. The moon, representing the female principle in counterpoint to the male sun, signifies chastity and mutability—both appropriate symbols for a young woman at this transitional age. The moon's waxing and waning, fullness and disappearance, are classic emblems of the stages of human life. As if to emphasize an allusion to change, Cassatt depicted two opposing crescents that resemble the conventional astronomical icons for the phases of the moon.

The decorative pattern formed by the driveway attests also to Cassatt's avid study of *ukiyo-e* prints. Further evidence of her adaptation of Japanese compositional strategies are the unconventional viewpoint, the cropping of the figure, the decorative spray of foliage at the upper right, and, most important, the treatment of space. Virtually eliminating the middle ground, Cassatt layered near and far as boldly as did Hiroshige. While many of her contemporaries merely used Asian props to announce their cosmopolitanism, Cassatt integrated the lessons of the Japanese printmakers with her own artistic impulses to create an original hybrid of East and West.

Cassatt employed a variety of means to create a poignant image of a young woman suspended between two stages of life. A delicate sense of loss emanates from her *Portrait of a Young Girl,* as the model's childhood and, with it, her unself-conscious rapport with nature are about to end.

1. Achille Segard, *Un Peintre des enfants et des mères, Mary Cassatt* (Paris: Librairie Paul Ollendorf, 1913), pp. 170–71; quoted in Natalie Spassky et al., *American Paintings in the Metropolitan Museum of Art,* vol. II, *A Catalogue of Works by Artists Born Between 1816 and 1845* (New York: The Metropolitan Museum of Art, 1985), p. 642.

2. For a discussion of Cassatt's Symbolism, see Judith A. Barter, "Mary Cassatt: Themes, Sources, and the Modern Woman," in Judith A. Barter et al., *Mary Cassatt: Modern Woman,* exhibition catalogue (Chicago: The Art Institute of Chicago, 1998), pp. 85–87 and 97–99.

Children in Woods, 1905

Oil on canvas, 32 × 30 inches
Bequest of Miss Adelaide Milton de Groot (1876–1967), 1967 (67.187.210)

This sun-filled painting depicts the artist's three daughters at their summer home on the island of North Haven, Maine. Eleanor, the oldest, recalled posing for such works: "When we were in North Haven, Papa would often have us put on our best white dresses and then ask us to sit in the grass or play in the woods. We thought it was so silly and the maids made such a fuss when they saw our clothes afterwards."[1]

Benson had made his debut as a plein-air painter in 1898 with a similar work, *In the Woods* (location unknown), depicting Eleanor and her brother George. From that time on, his children frequently posed for him, receiving fifteen cents an hour for the chore. Some of the paintings that resulted hint at the active life the family enjoyed in Maine; more often, the Benson youngsters appear passive and uncommunicative. In *Children in Woods*, the girls' downcast eyes suggest that they are reading. Benson often permitted his models this means of passing the time, but he usually hid the book, as he did here, to convey an impression of pure idleness.

The effort that Eleanor Benson considered "silly" resulted in a carefully structured composition that reflects both her father's academic training and his more recently adopted Impressionism. Demonstrating the devotion to strong design he had acquired at the School of the Museum of Fine Arts, Boston, and the Académie Julian in Paris, Benson arranged his daughters in three overlapping pyramids: seven-year-old Sylvia forms a small triangle at the left; fourteen-year-old Elisabeth (whose back is to the viewer) creates another, which is subsumed into the larger pyramid whose apex is fifteen-year-old Eleanor's blonde head.[2]

Benson's high-keyed palette, concern with light, and lively brushwork reveal his debt to Impressionism. Touches of pink, yellow, blue, and lavender shimmer in dresses and ribbons. The younger girls' auburn hair echoes the russet tones of the forest, integrating figures and setting. The initially startling contrast of pale frocks and dark trees is based on subtly orchestrated rhythms of light and shadow. A band of dappled shade crosses the lower portion of the canvas, intensifying the pink of Sylvia's dress and tinting Elisabeth's white frock mauve. Next, a streak of brilliant light warms Sylvia's head and Eleanor, who glows against the velvety background of spruce trees. Patches of sunlight dance among the evergreens, carrying the play of light into the densest shadow. Throughout the canvas, flickering brushstrokes capture the shifting effect of late-morning sunshine. Despite its spontaneous appearance, *Children in Woods* may have been executed in the studio from sketches Benson made in the open air. He worked only until noon on North Haven, reserving the afternoons for hiking, sailing, and fishing. Following standard academic procedure, he completed his summer canvases during the winter, using preliminary studies and photographs he had made outdoors.[3] Thus, this colorful record of a summer in Maine may have been painted during a snowy winter in Salem, Massachusetts.

A lifelong resident of Salem, Benson commuted into Boston to teach at the Museum School, where he had once studied. Together with his fellow faculty member and close friend Edmund C. Tarbell, he was identified as a member of the Boston school of Impressionists. The group, which also included Philip L. Hale, William MacGregor Paxton, and Joseph DeCamp, was noted for paintings of beautiful, privileged women at ease in sunny landscapes or tasteful interiors. Benson's paintings of his family represent a high point of Boston Impressionism. *Children in Woods* epitomizes his idyllic world of fine weather, well-mannered children, and an unblemished nature apparently invented for their recreation.

1. Quoted by Faith Andrews Bedford in Faith Andrews Bedford, Susan C. Faxon, and Bruce W. Chambers, *Frank W. Benson: A Retrospective,* exhibition catalogue (New York: Berry-Hill Galleries, 1989), p. 60. Ms. Bedford is the artist's great-granddaughter.

2. The identification of the sitters is based on an undated letter from Faith Andrews Bedford; object file, Department of American Paintings and Sculpture, The Metropolitan Museum of Art. Their ages are based on the 1900 census records.

3. Sheila Dugan, "Frank W. Benson," in *Ten American Painters,* exhibition catalogue (New York: Spanierman Gallery, 1990), p. 83.

39 F. LUIS MORA (1874–1940)

Flowers of the Field, 1913

Oil on canvas, 40 × 36 inches
Gift of Mr. and Mrs. Walter C. Crawford, 1967 (67.24)

"The smell of sweet grasses, clover blossoms and daisy fields still lingers in the flowers and around the young girls," a contemporary critic wrote of *Flowers of the Field,* adding, "This is a wholesome picture full of the quiet joy of young girlhood."[1] Mora painted this canvas at his country home in Gaylordsville, Connecticut. There, on July 11, 1913, he recorded in his diary the first of a series of wildflower still lifes he would execute before his return to New York in the early autumn. Sometime in August, apparently, he decided to combine flowers with the female figure—a pairing favored by many American Impressionists. Unfortunately, Mora's diary for the month of August is missing, but by early September, when his artist-friend Robert Nisbet came to see him, *Flowers of the Field* was completed. On September 8, the day after the visit, Mora noted in his diary that Nisbet had predicted that the work would "make a big noise" in the fall exhibitions. "I do hope it does," Mora wrote. "It looked fine yesterday—fresh as a daisy."[2]

Demonstrating his confidence in the painting, Mora sent it to the exhibition *Thirty Paintings by Thirty Artists* held at the Macbeth Gallery in November 1913. The response surely gratified him. The *New York Times* critic found *Flowers of the Field* "charming"; another called it "an excellent picture." *Art News* pronounced it "a thoroughly satisfactory canvas, skilful in modeling and in the psychology of happy childhood."[3] Several critics praised the work's appealing palette. Mora emphasized the multicolored blossoms by setting them against a neutral background and limiting the colors of the models' costumes. The blue-and-white dress of the seated girl echoes her limpid blue eyes and the embroidered tablecloth, while the deep pink dots on the white dress of the standing girl harmonize with the warmer colors within the bouquet. The artless floral arrangement exemplifies the diversity of hue and form that delighted Mora: Queen Anne's lace, black-eyed Susans, butter-and-eggs, yarrow, and a purple blossom (possibly joe-pye weed) mingle in the dented pewter pitcher.

Mora's *Flowers of the Field* was influenced by his teachers at the Boston Museum School, Frank W.

Benson and Edmund C. Tarbell. As Benson had done in *Children in Woods* (no. 38), Mora allied young girls with the freshness and simplicity of the natural world. Although he placed his models indoors, as Tarbell had done in *Across the Room* (no. 34), Mora evoked nature in the unstudied beauty of the wildflowers they are arranging. The unaffected country girls are also, he implies, flowers of the field. His punning title may have been intended to evoke the biblical passage, "Consider the lilies of the field, how they grow; they toil not, neither do they spin: And yet I say unto you, That even Solomon in all his glory was not arrayed like one of these" (Matt. 6:28–29).

In addition to such Impressionist works as *Flowers of the Field,* Mora produced genre paintings set in Spain and his native Latin America. Born in Montevideo, Uruguay, to a French mother and a Spanish father, he received his first art instruction at home. His father, the sculptor Domingo Mora, was director of the Museo Nacional de Bellas Artes. The family immigrated to the United States in 1880, eventually settling in Boston, where Luis Mora studied with Benson and Tarbell at the School of the Museum of Fine Arts. About 1892 he went to New York and enrolled at the Art Students League, where he studied under H. Siddons Mowbray. At the same time, he began working as a freelance illustrator for *Harper's Weekly;* he would eventually contribute drawings to *Scribner's Magazine* and the *Century* as well.

Mora embarked on a one-year tour of Europe in 1896. After a brief stop in Paris, he proceeded to Spain, where he visited relatives in Barcelona and copied the Spanish masterworks at the Prado in Madrid. That trip can be considered the completion of his professional training, although unlike the majority of his American predecessors, he never enrolled in a European academy. Revealing the increased cultural self-confidence of Americans after World War I, a journalist cited Mora in 1918 as "a successful exponent of the idea that artists need not go abroad for their formal training."[4]

1. Lorinda Munson Bryant, *American Pictures and Their Painters* (New York: John Lane Company, 1917), p. 227.

2. F. Luis Mora Papers, Archives of American Art, Smithsonian Institution, Washington, D.C., roll 3569, frames 110 and 122.

3. Macbeth Gallery Papers, Archives of American Art, Smithsonian Institution, Washington, D.C., roll NMc2, frames 167–71.

4. "Paintings by F. Luis Mora," *Country Life* 33 (February 1918), p. 57.

Selected Bibliography

GENERAL SOURCES

Fairbrother, Trevor J., et al. *The Bostonians: Painters of an Elegant Age, 1870–1930.* Exhibition catalogue. Boston: Museum of Fine Arts, 1986.

Folk, Thomas C. *The Pennsylvania Impressionists.* Madison, N.J.: Fairleigh Dickinson University Press; London: Associated University Presses, 1997.

Gerdts, William H. *American Impressionism.* New York: Abbeville Press, 1984. Includes an extensive bibliography.

————. *American Impressionism: Masterworks from Public and Private Collections.* Exhibition catalogue. Lugano-Castagnola, Switzerland: Thyssen-Bornemisza Foundation, 1990.

————. *Lasting Impressions: American Painters in France, 1865–1915.* Exhibition catalogue. Giverny: Musée Américain, 1992.

————. *Monet's Giverny: An Impressionist Colony.* New York: Abbeville Press, 1993.

Heisinger, Ulrich W. *Impressionism in America: The Ten American Painters.* Munich: Prestel-Verlag, 1991.

Larkin, Susan G. "'A Regular Rendezvous for Impressionists': The Cos Cob Art Colony, 1882–1920." Ph.D. dissertation. City University of New York, 1996.

————. *The Cos Cob Art Colony: Impressionists on the Connecticut Shore.* New Haven: National Academy of Design in association with Yale University Press, in press.

Meixner, Laura L. *An International Episode: Millet, Monet, and Their North American Counterparts.* Exhibition catalogue. Memphis, Tenn.: Dixon Gallery and Gardens, 1982.

Spencer, Harold, Susan G. Larkin, and Jeffrey W. Andersen. *Connecticut and American Impressionism.* Exhibition catalogue. Storrs: The University of Connecticut, 1980.

Ten American Painters. Exhibition catalogue. New York: Spanierman Gallery, 1990.

Weinberg, H. Barbara. *The Lure of Paris: Nineteenth-Century American Painters and Their French Teachers.* New York: Abbeville Press, 1991.

Weinberg, H. Barbara, Doreen Bolger, and David Park Curry. *American Impressionism and Realism: The Painting of Modern Life, 1885–1915.* Exhibition catalogue. New York: The Metropolitan Museum of Art, 1994. Includes an extensive bibliography.

MONOGRAPHS

Atkinson, D. Scott, and Nicolai Cikovsky, Jr. *William Merritt Chase: Summers at Shinnecock, 1891–1902.* Exhibition catalogue. Washington, D.C.: National Gallery of Art, 1987.

Barilleaux, René Paul, and Victoria J. Beck. *G. Ruger Donoho: A Painter's Path.* Jackson, Miss.: Mississippi Museum of Art, 1995.

Barter, Judith A., et al. *Mary Cassatt: Modern Woman.* Exhibition catalogue. Chicago: The Art Institute of Chicago, 1998.

Baur, John I. H. *Theodore Robinson, 1852–1896.* Exhibition catalogue. New York: The Brooklyn Museum, 1946. Reprinted in Baur, *Three Nineteenth-Century American Painters,* New York: Arno Press, 1969.

Burke, Doreen Bolger. *J. Alden Weir: An American Impressionist.* Newark: University of Delaware Press, 1983.

Colville, Thomas L. *Charles Harold Davis, N.A. 1856–1933.* Exhibition catalogue. Mystic, Conn.: Mystic Art Association, 1982.

Emerson, Sandra, Lucretia H. Giese, and Laura C. Luckey. *A. C. Goodwin, 1864–1929.* Exhibition catalogue. Boston: Museum of Fine Arts, 1974.

Folk, Thomas C. *Edward Redfield: First Master of the Twentieth-Century Landscape.* Exhibition catalogue. Allentown, Pa.: Allentown Art Museum, 1987.

———. *Walter Elmer Schofield: Bold Impressionist.* Exhibition catalogue. Chadds Ford, Pa.: Brandywine River Museum, 1983.

Heisinger, Ulrich W. *Childe Hassam: American Impressionist.* Munich and New York: Prestel, 1994.

Hill, May Brawley. *Grez Days: Robert Vonnoh in France.* Exhibition catalogue. New York: Berry-Hill Galleries, 1987.

Johnston, Sona. *Theodore Robinson, 1852–1896.* Exhibition catalogue. Baltimore: Baltimore Museum of Art, 1973.

Lowrey, Carol. "The Art of Philip Leslie Hale." In *Philip Leslie Hale, A.N.A., 1865–1931.* Exhibition catalogue. Boston: Vose Galleries, 1988.

Mathews, Nancy Mowll. *Mary Cassatt: A Life.* New York: Villard Books, 1994.

Peterkin, L. Denis, and Lionello Venturi. *An Exhibition of Oils and Pastels by Arthur C. Goodwin.* Exhibition catalogue. New York: Wildenstein Gallery, 1946.

Peters, Lisa N. *John Henry Twachtman: An American Impressionist.* Exhibition catalogue. Atlanta: High Museum of Art, 1999; distributed by Hudson Hills Press, New York.

———. "Twachtman's Greenwich Paintings: Context and Chronology." In Deborah Chotner, Lisa N. Peters, and Kathleen A. Pyne, *John Twachtman: Connecticut Landscapes.* Exhibition catalogue. Washington, D.C.: National Gallery of Art, 1990; distributed by Harry N. Abrams, New York.

Pisano, Ronald G. *A Leading Spirit in American Art: William Merritt Chase, 1849–1916.* Exhibition catalogue. Seattle: Henry Art Gallery, University of Washington, 1983.

———. *William de Leftwich Dodge: Impressions Home and Abroad.* Exhibition catalogue. New York: Beacon Hill Fine Art, 1998.

Pisano, Ronald G., and Ann C. Madonia. *Gifford Beal: Picture-Maker.* Exhibition catalogue. New York: Kraushaar Galleries, 1993.

Venturi, Lionello. *Arthur Clifton Goodwin.* Exhibition catalogue. Andover, Mass.: Addison Gallery of American Art, 1946.

Young, Dorothy Weir. *The Life and Letters of J. Alden Weir.* New Haven: Yale University Press, 1960. Reprint. New York: Kennedy Graphics and DaCapo, 1971.

Index of Artists

Numerals refer to catalogue numbers.

Theodore Robinson, *The Old Mill (Vieux moulin)* (detail), ca. 1892 (no. 9)